Gnosis and The Tarot

A Key to the Gnostic Path of Tarot

By

Melvin Harris

Copyright© 2016 by Melvin Harris
Rose Light Publications

All rights reserved.

DEDICATION

To my wife who has been and continues to be a True Friend, I dedicate this work with Love.

Victoria Harris

ACKNOWLEDGMENTS

It is said that a Tree is known by its fruit. It is my sincere wish that the present work reflects in some small measure the gratitude, appreciation and Love I have for:

The Stewards of the **Builders of the Adytum** past and present for their tireless work and service to Humanity by keeping the treasure entrusted to them "pure and undefiled" — L.V.X.

The International School of the Golden Rosycross — **Lectorium Rosicrucianum** — a *Gnostic Spiritual School*. Stewards of The Christian Mystery of Initiation of the Holy Rosycross for the New Era. The Young Gnostic Brotherhood.

REFERENCES

In conjunction with this work the following is suggested reading:

The Tarot — A key to the Wisdom of the Ages
by Paul Foster Case

The Book of Tokens by Paul Foster Case

The True and Invisible Rosicrucian Order
by Paul Foster Case

Dei Gloria Intacta by Jan van Rijckenborgh

The Coming New Man by Jan van Rijckenborgh

The Call of the Brotherhood of the Rosycross
by Jan van Rijckenborgh

Table of Contents

PREFACE	8
PRELIMINARY CONSIDERATIONS	11
FAITH	13
THE GREAT DECEPTION	17
FALSE PHROPETS	25
BELOW THE ANGELS	32
NO EMPTY SPACE	38
YOKE OF THE LAW	46
LIBERTY OF THE GOSPELS	52
GLORY OF GOD	58
THE GREATEST OF THESE	64
REVELATION	70
DOMINION	74
GRACE	78
WEALTH	84
FERTILITY	89

Table of Contents (continued)

WISDOM	95
PEACE	99
LIFE	103
FIRST PROCEDURE	107
SECOND PROCEDURE	114
THIRD PROCEDURE	120
ROSE LIGHT METHOD	126
ORACLE METHOD	149
IMPLICATIONS OF HEBREW LETTERS	156
IMPLICATIONS OF MINOR ARCANA	164
ABOUT THE AUTHOR	170

PREFACE

The present work is offered to all who may be sincerely interested in the original and true purpose of divination using the Tarot.

In this current age of greed, gross materialism and selfishness there are unfortunately very few who have time for or much interest in the sacred Mysteries.

Tarot divination is not fortune telling and needs to be approached, not with that kind of levity and irreverent attitude common among practitioners of fortune telling, but with respect due to the obvious sublime Wisdom with which the Tarot is adorned as well as the powerful (invisible) forces which control their orientation when they are properly used under the right conditions for these forces to act. This one requirement disqualifies all carnival and house party settings which are the favored accommodations of pretenders. It is simply not possible for any individual who does not have clear, objective insight into the workings of their own thought processes to be able to understand that of another much less be of help or offer guidance. "Good intentions" — so called — have no place in the motives of one who proposes to divine for themselves much less for another individual.

This is advanced use of Tarot, and the chief use of the methods described herein are to help you in the work of personality transmutation and thus enable you to become a living channel for the transmission of true guidance from — the Higher — the Divine — the Primal Will-to-Good.

Rose Light is a method of tarot Divination based on the Teachings of the Western Mystery Tradition as contained in the Holy Qabalah, Sacred Tarot and the Gnosis. Fortune telling fosters fatalism and breeds superstition. Divination provides guidance based on Divine Law, leading to Self-knowledge —to Gnosis. To debase the Sacred Art of divination through fortune telling is missing the mark. The consequences are grave, keeping in mind the Law "As you sow, so shall you reap."

If one's state of life is such that one must ask a fortune teller — if a partner or spouse is faithful — or whether or not to do or say something to the boss — or will one inherit vast sums of money, a fortune teller will be of no real help. The same result will be achieved by asking a complete and total stranger to take control of one's life.

It is a great delusion to think that it is possible to control or change future events and circumstances by being forewarned, thus preparing oneself in advance. Especially considering the fact that one is unable to deal with the present situation or circumstance.

Divination, based on Divine Law, is an Art that enables the individual to make contact with and come into an awareness of his/her own inner guide and tribunal [conscience] so that there is no longer any delusion concerning one's circumstances and experiences in life.

For the preliminary study of the Rose Light divination system it is crucial that you follow the instructions carefully. This method does not suit anyone who is in a hurry to learn the "trick" to reading tarot cards or showing others what they "know" about Tarot. It is imperative that you keep a diary or a record of all readings.

LUX SANCTA — LUX LIBERTAT

SOME PRELIMINARY CONSIDERATIONS

Use of the word Gnosis in this work has the meaning — knowledge of spiritual mysteries and is based on the meaning of the Greek word for knowledge. Not in theory but via experience do we come to know anything of the spiritual mysteries. The greatest mystery of which is "Man Know Thyself!"

Use of the word Divination refers to — discovery via insight and intuition, knowledge of the Divine Self, the Spirit-soul human being.

A minimum of five months is required to learn the Rose Light divination method. This method is not for answering specific questions or any similar approach. The Art of divination using the sacred Tarot and the Rose Light method is a way to access the oracle of your own Soul.

Christ Hierophant refers to the Triumphant and Eternal Intelligence, the true revealer of the Mysteries and the source of Wisdom.

Where the term "Victory Work" is used it has the same meaning as the "Great Work."

The Tarot images are from the Rose Light deck.

All images used in this work are © Melvin Harris, MelvinHarrisArt.com, & ArtbyMelvin.com

THE AMEN / 11

FAITH

(The Amen)

"These things saith the Amen, the faithful and true witness, the beginning of the creation of God—to the Victor will I grant to sit with me in my throne..."

Through the Amen spiritual powers are increased because spiritual virtues are deposited and augmented therein. All dwellers on earth are under its shadow. To possess the power of The Amen is to be able to "subdue the most ferocious animals" and be able to "pronounce the words which paralyze and charm serpents." The Amen is Divine Will operating through The Christos.

"...Not mine but, the Will of the father.."

To know the Will of the Father is to know all the reality of the Primordial Wisdom. Will prepares all created beings, each individually, for the demonstration of the existence of the Primordial Glory. To possess the Will of the Father is to be acquainted with the laws of perpetual motion, and to be in a position to demonstrate the quadrature of the circle. Yod is the path whereby the beneficence and loving-kindness of the One Self finds expression through the central Ego. In human consciousness Yod manifests as the power of mutual attraction between bodies and is what governs their joining.

The Will of God is the sole motivating Force in all Creation. Individuals who do not understand this respond to the Touch of Divine Will in an erroneous manner. When the center of an individual's consciousness is focused in the personality, that person cannot recognize that the sense of personal volition and will he is experiencing, really transcends his individual personality. What such an individual experiences as his own drive to accomplish and his own will to be, is in truth the Divine Will manifesting.

"...and this is the Victory that overcometh the World..."

The work of purifying the desire-nature is the work of all who yearn for the Light. Control of mental imagery is the key to the door of the Higher Wisdom. The quality of imagery improves as the desire-nature is purged of the dross of hidden guilt. In the Light of the Self-Image the One Energy is realized as Divine Love and this realization renders one receptive to the influence of Wisdom and Love that is centered in Christos.

The ability to create images that reflect the Higher Wisdom, depends upon realizing that the Procreative Energy is sacred. This is the Energy that perpetuates all of Creation and it is what allows you to maintain your physical existence. It is what will free you from the confines of materiality when you learn its Secret. This Energy is what the Alchemists called the "Secret Fire."

"Do not be conformed to this world, but be transformed by the renewing of your minds, so that you may discern what is the Will of God – what is the good and acceptable and perfect Will of God."

This message provides a key to the path that leads to liberation for one who is in bondage to this world because of I-centered thinking, and one who is totally immersed in materiality.

Natural man is chained to delusion and does not see that he is deluded; he judges everything based on surface appearances. He is "conformed to this world."

If we are to be free from bondage to the wheel of birth and death, we are to have a renewal of our minds. We must come to see our own foolishness. A new thinking faculty must develop that is able to perceive the divine plan of salvation for those in bondage, and to utilize the force of the spiritual sun to help carry out that divine plan and to bring that plan to fulfillment.

LUX SANCTA — LUX LIBERTAT

THE ARCHON / 15

THE GREAT DECEPTION

The world is in a state of great crisis. Humanity as a whole faces a turning point. There will be no attempt made in these writings to emphasize the current suffering of Humankind in order to depress the reader and thus elicit acceptance of this work via guilt manipulation. The present condition of world stress requires that the author be clear and exact as to the nature of what is occurring in the world and its cause.

Humanity is at the end of a Life-cycle and at the ushering in of a new era. Man is being called to return to his divine Homeland and claim his birthright in the true Kingdom of Light. Through ignorance, Humankind has succeeded in alienating itself from its true and original nature. Through ignorance, man has misused a divine gift and reaped some most undesirable results.

Man himself is the cause of the present climate of crisis in the world; it is not "fate" nor is it the will of some "vengeful God" as is believed by the deluded. It is a fundamental part of the teaching of a Mystery School and the School stands firm on this point: man himself is the author of his own life-story.

Acceptance of this point is vital, when understood. This fact becomes the basis of support for all of the work of personality transmutation, and the subsequent transformation of the entire being.

"Man, know Thyself" has been echoed through all the ages by the wise and it has been maintained that knowledge of the Self is the key to gaining dominion in one's life. However, there are still too few who can say, "Yes, truly the Self is known. The King has been seen." There are still too few who even know where to look for the true Self, the King of Light. Centered in each living being is the source of all wisdom, love and knowledge waiting to come forth. But in most, and by far too many, the way has not been prepared for the King to return to His throne.

Observing our surroundings, it is easy to witness the constant ebb and flow of alternating activity and rest. It matters not whether it is the motion of the stars, the life cycles of plants or human life that is being considered; all are subject to the process of birth, zenith, decline and death. There is nothing and no one in manifestation exempt from this process.

The law of manifest existence is exact. Everything has its time, season, appointed sphere of operation, limit and boundary of expression. Man, for the most part, is ignorant of his true place in this process and believes himself to be threatened by this beneficent working of divinity. Because man fears the unknown, all of nature appears to be an enemy. Operating from the premise that the processes of life are inimical to him, man devotes all of his efforts and energies into fighting life instead of living life.

Ignorance and fear have man convinced that all of his suffering is due to the actions of some angry and vengeful god, punishing him for some "sin" committed by his ancestors. This thinking is a carry-over from the old dispensation where primitive and materialistic concepts of the sacred writings were projected into the astral sphere of this material plane. On the surface, life does appear to be cruel and unjust and man does seem to be a hopeless victim of fate subject to the whims of chance. This is only an appearance. Acceptance of this appearance is based on man's misinterpretation of life and his relationship to the entire life process.

Do not be in despair over suffering; do not let afflictions vex you; pain is the touch of the Divine and the teacher of the soul. The processes of the material sphere do appear to be in opposition to man, but in truth, it is a merciful gift that nothing is permanent in this sphere. Man has fallen from grace, and there is no real evidence to dispute this fact even considering all of man's great achievements.

The grace of which ROSE LIGHT speaks is not some sort of imagined spiritual "torte" which one earns for being good. It is an actual state of consciousness long forgotten by most. In an individual who is in a state of grace, there is neither trace of any sense of personal volition nor concern over what to do. All acts are the work of the Father; all volition is the Will of the Father. To be in grace is to know the meaning of the teaching, "My Father worketh and I work."

In this light, the words of the apostle, "Know ye not that ye are the temple of the Living God and that the spirit of God dwells within you?" takes on new meaning. We are the residence of the power that created all that exists--the very breath of God abides within our being. Being made in the image and likeness of the Creator, we have powers and abilities akin to the nature of our divine parent. This is at once the root and cause of our present dilemma as well as the key and means to our achieving conscious union with God.

Man, for the most part, has fallen from grace. He has eaten from the Tree of the Knowledge of Good and Evil. The fruit of this tree is this earth and the good and evil are the dual expressions of the seven forces and vibrations of light and sound which interact upon one another and surround and control the four planes of existence which constitute the physical universe.

A consequence of Man's experiencing the tree of the knowledge of good and evil is that it has made him intoxicated and therefore unconscious so that he is no longer aware of his true identity. He is in a nightmare from which he cannot awaken. He fights desperately to maintain his life because he does feel immortal, but this feeling is only a faint specter in the far recesses of his memory experienced as desire to be free from his prison of death. He is bound to the laws of his own ignorance and has become a beast-man, a wanderer in the wasteland, stalking and preying on his fellow man.

The Ancients wrote, "All is Mind. The universe is mental. God meditates the universe into existence. In Him we live, move and have our being." All these thoughts center around one premise: the oneness of God and the unity of all life. There is only one God. From this premise it is clear to see that there can be no one thing that exists other than God or outside of God, for then it would have another source of origin and this would instantly negate the validity of a single deity.

Thus, anything we perceive as separate and singular must be so within a relative frame of reference, that frame of reference being within the consciousness of God. Whatever substance we believe we have or think we experience, it is the substance of God. There is only one God.

All indeed would be lost were it not for the sacrifice of a great Soul. This divine being is in this plane of manifestation but does not "eat of its fruit." His presence is experienced as light. This is not some metaphysical or mystical imagining, nor is it any psychic experience conjured up via various occult methods. This light is of such a nature that it can only be recognized through a vehicle of perception capable of sustaining its vibration. In most of Humankind, this vehicle is no more than a vestige, a mere trace of what it once was. This vehicle is in a state of such atrophy because most of Humankind has tried to sustain the vibration of this sphere of corruptible, finite substance in a vehicle fashioned to be the residence of the King.

Man — living within the mind of God, fashioned from the substance of divinity, made in the image and likeness of God — has a definite role to play in the Divine Plan. The true Light of Grace cannot be seen by any who cling to the darkness of separative, materialistic, self-gratifying personal desires and I-centered thinking.

"Light has come into the world" declare the sacred writings and because Light is in this world, man can succeed if he does the work. When man stops fighting to maintain and hold on to the "things of this world" (the degenerative vibration of this material plane) and discards this vehicle in exchange for the Body of Christos, he begins the work of return.

As with all things in this world, proper preparation is the key to desired results. The instruction offered by the ROSE LIGHT serves only as an aid--the student must do the work. The ancients declared, "When the student is ready, the teacher will appear." In not so ancient times, it was stated thus, "You can lead a horse to water, but you cannot make him drink." This will ever be the case. Even now, as whoever it is who reads these words will know, when it is said, "Our divine inheritance is our ability to create mental images and it is the key to our true liberation," only those who are prepared to understand and make use of this information will do so.

Even more, whatever images hold our attention on a continual basis do and will manifest in our daily experience. This is at the basis of all our problems. We are not separate beings. But as long as we believe we have a need to take from another in order to have security, we will create the images that support this delusion and we will continue to suffer the consequences. There is no separate, omnipotent demon with powers to thwart God's Will; there is only one God. Our problems are the makings of our inability to create images that reflect the reality of life — the oneness of God — the unity of all life. This is the reality as seen by all the great guides of humanity.

Our individual consciousness is a focusing point for the Divine Light which is experiencing manifestation through particular soul consciousnesses. Inability to perceive that we are not the originating point for our sense of volition causes us to suppose that we have nothing to depend upon for our true sense of security except our own inadequate personalities. This leads us to imagine that we are in danger of extinction unless we destroy our enemies first, no matter if these enemies be real or imagined, political or economic, racial or religious. This is the Great Deception, the grand lie that has Humankind in its present dilemma.

Centered within man is the potential to know and express the same creative intelligence that maintains all of manifest existence. Within man is the ability to control the forces of life so that he might transform his environment and bring the fulfillment of the prayer, "Thy Will be done on earth as it is in Heaven."

The ROSE LIGHT exists to aid and serve the student who has entered upon the Way of Return. With the light of Divine Consciousness, the veils of ignorance are penetrated and a way to gain the strength necessary to control the forces of this sphere is seen.

Following the guidance of ROSE LIGHT one may become a house of the living God, be free from the chains of ignorance and suffering, and have the consciousness renewed through the light of Grace.

IPSISSIMUS / 9

FALSE PROPHETS

A most harmful side effect of eating from the Tree of the Knowledge of Good and Evil (being incarnate in the physical plane) is the delusion that the personality-being is a separate, autonomous entity. It is the belief in a completely separate, independent being with a will all its own. Because of this belief all experiences are placed in one of two categories, the first being good, and the second evil. Good is mainly anything which brings physical gratification and comfort. Whatever brings pain and discomfort or defeats the will is classed under the heading of evil. If the majority of life experiences are painful and filled with suffering and marked with defeated desires, one will see himself as being surrounded by evil.

The inability to recognize the unity of all life is the chain that binds to the delusion of separation. While in this dream state, unable to awaken to the reality of the Light, there are nonetheless certain powers and abilities which if utilized correctly would lead to liberation and release from the chains of delusion.

Humankind — as a child of God, has a certain inherited potential or gifts. When undeveloped, these gifts are no more than a mere caricature of the faculties the Rose Man, who walks in Grace, possesses. The ability to generate mental images is one such gift — a gift that is of the same nature as the divine power that created this universe. The inherent ability to create mentally and generate images is the key to liberation and the cause of bondage.

The personality-being believes himself to be a separate, autonomous entity and will act and imagine accordingly. So long as he believes he is surrounded by enemies and must fight — taking from another in order to have peace and security — he will create images and therefore circumstances to support this delusion and thereby suffer the consequences. Misuse of this ability — due to ignorance — has resulted in the generation of images of envy, mistrust, jealousy, hate and a legion of other atrocities.

Yet, he is still blind to the image of the Rose Man which sorely needs his life-giving attention. He stands a prisoner in the fortress of separation, fashioned by his own images, strengthened by his persistence in error. There is no hope — save that he be blasted from his castle of self-importance and that the delusion of greatness be destroyed. He cannot see that the key to release is within his grasp.

Living an I-centered, self-serving life is not living in a state of Grace. If an individual recognizes this fact, there arises a desire for release and liberation from what most assuredly seems like a cruel and unjust process, whether it be an aspect of divinity or not.

There may be an earnest desire to make amends and live a just life, but there is also a strong feeling of inadequacy due to the realization of the real state of ignorance that the individual is in. It soon becomes evident that one will require help and guidance in order to be released from the prison of materialism and awakened from the nightmare of separation.

Even help and guidance will not be enough if the individual is not prepared to receive it. This is a fact as taught in the Hermetic writings, "when the student is ready, the teacher will appear." Preparing to receive help is the first work of an individual who wishes to be victorious.

This preliminary work involves purification of the mental and emotional as well as physical expressions that are experienced as the personality. It involves discovering the deception of separatism and banishing the false prophets of personal will.

The premise that the personality-being is a separate, autonomous entity, has led to a most erroneous conclusion. The key to release is truly within reach. The continued belief that one has only his personality upon which to depend in order to deal with life's events, destroys any hope and prevents him from seeing any way out.

We are one in divinity. There is no separation. There is no will save the divine Will of the All. The person who wishes to become victorious must call these facts to mind continually and repeatedly until all thoughts, speech and actions portray this truth.

Making this thought a part of memory and incorporating it into the responses to life, will bring about a gradual change in the individual's point of view and a gradual — yet steady and continuous — influx of spiritual Light. This will result in a definite awakening or quickening of the consciousness. By continually imaging a spiritual reality and focusing the attention on the unity of life, one begins to have experiences that support this fact. Recognition of the illusion of personal will brings all life's activities into a new light and all is begun to be seen as the will of God manifest. There also comes the realization and the awakening that what appears to be a sense of personal power and volition is really an unenlightened response to the touch of God.

Man has identified himself with the ever-shifting, continuous, cyclic manifestations of life and therefore perceives himself to be doomed to eternal imprisonment in the web of futility. When, by the awakening of a sincere desire, man begins to remember his divine heritage and unity with God, certain faculties in his consciousness which have been quite dormant are brought into activity. With these awakened perceptions comes a more vivid recognition of the unity of all life--a realization that no thought, word or action is private, separate or unrelated to anyone or anything else. With this awakening comes also the knowledge that we are joined to error as well as truth. As we are not alone in our thinking, feeling and doing, we most certainly cannot expect anyone else to be exempt from this. We are all within the mind of God. All the immature, unripe images fashioned by an ignorant humanity exist within the universal substance, and man has drawn upon and elaborated them with great efficiency.

The wisdom and power that created the entire cosmos is centered within man. All knowledge, Truth and Light may be contacted at the center of Man. As the alchemist stated, "what thou seekest, truly thou art that." Remember, the personality-self with which most of humanity identifies is not the center of wisdom and power mentioned above. Immature, untransmuted personalities are at the basis of all problems facing man. The universal substance is replete with knowledge concerning one thing or another that is exciting, intriguing, often quite mysterious, yet has nothing to do with the work-of transmutation save that it serves as a warning about the dangers of believing such nonsense.

We possess a divine faculty of cognition that when awakened and developed, will enable us to know all there is to know about anything without having to ask another or consult a book. In most of humanity, this faculty is still buried and smothered by the erroneous actions of selfishness, so infected by the poison of fear, hate and envy; it is only a testimony to the incorruptibility of spirit that such a faculty still survives.

Preparation to receive help from the Inner Voice, the true Teacher, involves discovering the deception of separative thinking. The individual must call to mind continually the fact that God is unity. There is no place outside of God. Centered in each one of us is the same Wisdom and Light that spawned the cosmos. At the very heart of us resides the true Spiritual Being, the one guide, the one true Teacher.

As the type of images generated begins to change — in response to the recognition of the Law of Unity — one's sense of identity will shift its center of focus and an alignment with the Central Self of all Humanity is made possible.

Persistence in this effort initiates the process of interior illumination. This illumination emanates from the divine Spirit-spark which has now begun to glow with an increased brilliance because it has been fed by images that speak of the Unity of life, the true reality of this Life-process.

As this imaging process continues, the state of ignorance diminishes and the dark areas of our being become light-filled until finally, in a flash, we are released from our self-imposed prisons of delusion and error.
We are put in touch with the source of all knowledge and the Light of this knowledge and wisdom guides us toward our goal and divine destiny of conscious union with God.

When this guidance is followed, the strife and turmoil of life begin to subside and a certain peace is established in its place.

Once centered in this peace — walking in the guidance of divine Light and freed from the prisons of falsehood — one is prepared to make an accurate assessment of his present situation and what it is that needs correcting in order that he might fulfill his destiny.

THE KINGDOM / 10

BELOW THE ANGELS

"What is man, that Thou art mindful of him?"
"Man, know thyself!"

One heartfelt question and one compelling declaration — both of them concern the Great Mystery. With the many advances in parapsychology and metaphysical thinking in general, much has been written about "Man" which can only lead to confusion when a very basic truth is forgotten. Phenomena in and of itself is not causal; it is the effect and not the source of origin. All experiences on the material plane of expression are the end result of the interplay and interchange of totally trans-personal forces operating at a much higher and more subtle level of the God-being.

What most people feel at ease to call "I" or their personalities is really only their imperfect and clouded response to the activities of the One Intelligence or the One Identity centered in a particular focus in order to gather the requisite knowledge or experience in this particular incarnation.

Contrary to what may be believed, Man is not divine offspring because he possesses a reasoning faculty. The ability to order and classify data gathered from sensory stimuli and to distinguish and discern differences and similarities also does not qualify Man for God-hood either. What "elevates" Man to the status of God-ling is the inherent ability to create and generate mental images which bring forth new and unique applications and manifestations of the laws of nature.

These images, having been previously arranged and classified by alert observation and accurate assessment are then remembered in response to a particular situation, thought or emotion. With the ability to create mentally, man can bring into manifestation any desired condition which was previously nonexistent. Unfortunately, the majority of Humankind bring into manifestation those images which are a direct response to the acceptance of the appearance of separateness. We are not separate, yet at the same time, we experience variation and diversity as a course of life. It is evident that we must discern just where it is we are in the scheme of things as well as what we are.

It must be stated again that the Man spoken of here is not the accepted concept as put forth by science. The Man referred to is the Universal Self, the Grand Adam of the Ancients, the Heavenly Man of the Apocalypse or Humanity in a generic sense.

It requires an inner clarity in one's ability to recognize an apparent order — to what before seemed to be complete chaos — in the manifested world and in the individual as well. This inner clarity allows one to begin to grasp the significance of his environment and to perceive a definite law in operation. Perception develops into a knowledge of nature which before was veiled — what once was dark, unknown and therefore threatening — is now recognized as the workings of the Divine Law.

This knowledge aids in the release from the

fear of life which held one captive. This release is experienced as an intensifying of inner peace and calm.

This experience is the result of remembering our divine heritage and that we are one with God. Seated in this calm, it is possible to discern the true relationship and relatedness of what appears to be antagonistic circumstances and conditions. There is a balance and harmony everywhere. The knowledge that the Law of Unity is ever in operation dispels the notion that one is a victim of a vengeful god or a cruel twist of fate. The universe is ordered; its workings and operations can be discerned and comprehended when the proper vantage point is known.

Life is continually bringing forth new issue, building up, tearing down and eliminating. This holds true for this singular planet as well as for our solar systems, galaxies and universes. The law of manifest being is seen to be a cyclic activity of continually rising, shining, fading and declining. There is nothing occurring in manifest creation which is not subject to this law.

Everything which is born must die and what dies is replaced — this too dies and is replaced — in a seeming unending cycle of repetition. Yet one must be on guard against forming an erroneous conclusion from this observation. Do not think of the Self as being the physical body — along with the intellectual, emotional and subjective nature — we are not that. All of these are subject to death.

One might ask: "If there be only one God — and in Him we live, move and have our being — how can it be that we die?" Our true Self does not die! For the true Self was "Born of God". The Ancients declared: "Man is the only Son of God and there is no God but Man." Man is the mediator for the Divine, Infinite Intelligence — the Universal Spirit which is known by the illumined to be God thinking Himself into being. By utilizing the Divine gift of mental creation, Man can control and have dominion in life.

When one begins to truly grasp the operations and the movements of life — and to perceive their significance — the images generated by the individual become more in harmony with the reality of life. There is no longer fear of the unknown. The law of cause and effect is recognized and the outcome of certain activities set into motion becomes predictable. As a result of this recognition there develops a true ability to discern just what kind of images and therefore activities one creates or initiates. The increasing inner radiance of the true Self of all, is now better able to express itself through a particular individual because the individual is cooperating with the process and not fighting some unknown enemy.

The individual becomes wise as to what not to image lest it manifest. Affirming the unity of life in thought, word and action allows one to stop craving for personal gratification of desires. There is no separation, no true lack; what is lacking is Man's ability to perceive this fact.

We are "but little lower than the angels." The "angels" are the creative powers of God which in and of themselves are characteristic of the fundamental qualities of Divinity as expressed and experienced in this particular life-cycle. Man is but a little lower than the powers of Omnipotence Itself — there is nothing that can exist on the same level as Godhead and still experience itself as being something other. Man is seen to be the primal or initial projection of God as a recognition of God's own potential.

The ability to analyze, experience and observe phenomena are possible because of this primary projection of the Infinite Intelligence into manifestation. The destruction of the delusion of separation and the recollection of the unity of life is in direct response to the influx of the universal Light Substance streaming from the One Identity.

The freedom from bondage to life circumstances and the wisdom to create a life in harmony with God come as a consequence of responding to the touch of the Divine Will. Our true place in life is much grander than can ever be imagined by anyone who is still bound and chained to the error of separative thinking, feeling and doing. We are truly "Crowned with glory," and we have dominion over the works of God.

ÆTH / 17

NO EMPTY SPACE

"Seek ye first the Kingdom of God."

There is a point of view concerning the nature of Creation and all of manifestation that states the world is evil and that no real good can ever come from this world. That to want to maintain this Life-process and all it entails is wrong and evil. This view sees the cyclic processes of the One Life-Power in manifestation as a cruel and torturous experience.

A second view-point on this subject, states this World and all it contains is God in manifestation and therefore cannot be anything other than what God intended — "And God said it was Good."

The true purpose of Creation has been a subject of contemplation for Humanity since the beginning of this current Life-cycle. There are many theories put forth as to the reason for the existence of this World as well as Humanity's place in the entire scheme. The tradition of the Rose and Cross, affirms the truth that Creation is for the purpose of experience. All that exists is the result of God contemplating His/Her own Self-potential. As individuals, we each are the means for this experiencing to take place.

In terms of time and space in manifestation, Creation has existed for ages; it is an ongoing cyclic process of birth, growth, decline, and death, an ever-turning wheel holding the fortune of Humanity in its grasp. Yet this process is not as inimical as it might seem at first glance, for each turn of the wheel rises to a higher level than the previous turn and each cycle of manifestation is on a higher level than the last.

This process of periodicity and alternation between activity and rest is a constant in the Life-Process. Its significance is both simple and profound at the same time. One cannot always be active — one must rest or fatigue will take over and force the issue. If an individual remains inactive for too long a period, atrophy results and exercise is the only remedy. Balance is the key to Victory, the Middle Way is the way to attainment.

God is omnipresent, the Kingdom of God is likewise everywhere. As individuals we each are God in expression, all at various levels yet God in expression none the less, God experiencing His/Her Creation through us. Seek the Kingdom of God within, for in truth, your physical vehicle is the intended Kingdom for the God in you. One has only to look at the health of the average person to see that very few people hold this view about their bodies.

The Great Work begins and ends on the physical plane and is completed on the same plane. This is a great Mystery. No member of the True Inner Invisible Order of the Rose and Cross seeks to escape Life. The discovery of the Kingdom of God requires a reversal in the thinking of the individual seeker. To discover the Kingdom one must have surrendered totally to the Will of God and abandoned any notion of separate personal autonomy. To depend upon the finite capabilities of the personal ego is to accept defeat.

The wise depend upon the One Will and are bound to serve and administer that Will in all the affairs of Life.

When the Unity of Life is not perceived, the delusion of separation prevails and thus one is unable to see the true connection that exists between the individual and the environment. All the large bodies of water on this planet intermingle in one way or another. Winds blow and carry the air around the globe, the earth shifts and moves regularly, the light of the sun is shared by all; we all breath the same air, drink the same water and live on the same earth. In truth we are a corporate being.

Science has shown — what had been taught for centuries by the Inner Schools — that all the elements that are found in the earth, are contained in the physical body and that in truth we are each a replica in miniature of the World we inhabit.

The Four Elements of the Alchemists are the four archetypal subdivisions of the One Substance that constitute our physical existence and environment; their Fire, Water, Air and Earth can be compared to the radiant energy, liquid, gas and solids of physics. Of greater importance is that these Four Elements represent four actual planes of existence and consciousness that are to be under the control of the individual when the Great Work is completed.

The Kingdom of God may only be entered by the straight and narrow gate; it is approached by a path that declines neither to the left nor to the right. The evil and materialistic cannot enter the Kingdom because for them to gaze upon the Face of the Anointed is to see only the darkness and terror of their own misdeeds as well as the degree of their bondage to the wheel of materiality. Those who live a life of "good" cannot enter the Kingdom because for them the fate of John the Baptist is yet ahead, and thus living a life of so-called good does not free the individual from the grip of death. The Christ Hierophant wisely instructed that "Among those that are born of women there hath not risen a greater than John the Baptist; but he that is least in the Kingdom of God is greater than he."

It is only by the intervention of a Higher Spiritual Force that the individual is enabled to enter the Kingdom of God. This Higher Genius manifests in the individual as the presence of the Christ Hierophant — continually instructing, guiding, and sometimes prodding the individual along the Path. It is the Christ Hierophant who instructs the individual in the proper actions to take that enable the individual to overcome his bondage to the Four Elements.

Freedom from the Wheel of Birth and Death, and the necessity to incarnate, requires a grasp, a comprehension of the Law at work behind the veil of outward appearance. The fourfold composition of manifest existence is referred to in many and various writings. It is explained in Qabalistic terminology as the Four Worlds: Atziluth, Briah, Yetzirah, and Assiah. Each of these Worlds represents a symbolic subdivision of the One Consciousness into distinct levels of expression and activity.

Atziluth is seen as the archetypal world, the plane of Spirit, the world of Divine ideas, the causal plane. The Fire of the Alchemist and Mystic is the energy of the world of Atziluth. This is the Sacred Fire, the fire that does not burn or consume, but is Life-imparting and regenerating.

Briah, the world of creativity and imagery, is the polar opposite of Atziluth. In Briah the seed-ideas of Atziluth are received and given a specific image. The Mystic Water is the energy of the world of Briah. It is the Water of Life which does not wet the hand, but which quenches the soul's thirst and renews the mind.

In Yetzirah, the consequence of the electric, projective, free energy of Atziluth interacting with the magnetic, receptive, confining force of Briah manifests. Thus, it is the world of ever shifting, turbulent, violently powerful energy. It is the pattern world, it is where all thoughts manifest as "things" and where they have an actual existence. The Magical Air is the energy of Yetzirah.

Assiah is the world of doing and manifesting; it is where the final result of the initial intent of Atziluth is realized. Assiah is the material universe and all of manifested creation. The energy of Assiah is the power to solidify the volatile, whirlwind force of Yetzirah, giving form and existence to the patterns of that world. The Invisible Earth is the energy of Assiah.

All of these four levels of energy express through you. The Great Work involves becoming consciously aware of the nature of this energy as it expresses through you — to safely direct the flow of this energy for the purification and consecration of your body in preparation for the Great Work.

The Kingdom of God is hidden from those who are not dedicated to its discovery. The way that leads to the Kingdom is a path traveled by a relative few. Only those who have been initiated by the Christ Hierophant are instructed in the Mysteries of the Kingdom of God. It is the Christ Hierophant who instructs the student on the ways and means to control the elemental nature and to prepare for his own individual initiation by the Christ.

The first step of preparation for the Great Work involves gaining control over the physical vehicle. It is a process that involves mental and physical exercises. An unprepared physical vehicle cannot withstand the subtle yet intense energy of the higher and inner realms.

The word kingdom implies dominion. The Work involves gaining dominion over the kingdom of his physical vehicle and to establish the reign of the true King. It is only through sacrifice of every attachment to the material that one may attain to dominion over the elemental nature. It takes work, patience, persistence and most important, unselfish service to all of Life. It is in this manner that the "spell" of the elements is broken and control is returned to the awakened individual.

Through work, the lethargy and inertia of the unbalanced expression of the Invisible Earth as well as the avarice and greed that also manifest as a result of the imbalance are overcome. Patience is the key to controlling the volatile, dynamic, lightening-like force of the Magical Air. Through sacrifice, the individual learns the sobering reality of the consequences of forming emotional attachments unwisely. These are a sign of the turbulent, troubled stirring of the Mystical Water. It is only in service to others that the flame of the Sacred Fire is able to burn away the dross of pride and egotism.

The limitations and restrictions of the physical plane become the doorway to the Kingdom of God when one is master of his elemental nature. It is through contact with the limiting, confining energy of the physical plane that each soul is able to work on perfecting the vehicle that will ultimately be the dwelling place of a Rose Man, the heaven born creature, the New Adam. While an individual is still deluded by the illusion of separation, that individual is a slave to the elemental nature and all of life is a prison. The individual who suffers from no such delusion, has dominion over the elemental nature and all of life is a Cosmic Dance of joy.

THE FOURTH HOUR / 18

YOKE OF THE LAW

CONSEQUENCES

"Consider the cost, whether ye have sufficient to finish"

In this present age of credit cards, machines that surrender cash on demand and the overall rush for instant gratification, the admonition from the Christ Hierophant to "consider the cost" — of ones actions — falls upon deaf ears. The majority of Humankind is engrossed in materialistic thinking — intoxicated with the lust for personal power — there is no awareness of the value of examining and evaluating thoughts, speech and actions.

Many are bound by a craving for things. This craving is experienced physically, psychically, emotionally and mentally and it expresses or manifests as the primary motivation fueling ideas of success or accomplishment. Whoever manages to accumulate the largest amount of material wealth, this is the one who is considered most successful; this is the one who is seen as an accomplisher.

What is done with this monetary abundance whether it be used for personal or "charitable" purposes, is overshadowed by and secondary to the fact that it is a trap. For it can only serve to hold one's thoughts to — obtaining more of it — managing more of it — keeping more of it and thus the individual is eternally bound to seek more of it.

It is not the scope of this work to prove or disprove the idea of reincarnation. It is, however, necessary to say that believe or not, an incarnation is too precious to waste on getting 'things' while the true value of being incarnate is passed over. Most seekers after Truth encounter their first true obstacle when they are confronted with the idea of abandoning materialistic thinking and they rationalize instead of reason. They refuse to put first things first and thus, as the Christ Hierophant points out, they fail — to their discredit and unfortunately, to the dishonor of some well meaning establishment or school.

The Great Work is a path which leads to dominion in the life of the individual who walks it. Through the operation of the Law of Unity a process begins which involves the elimination entirely of all thoughts, words and actions which are seen to be not in harmony with this law. It is a process which begins the restructuring and the reorganization of the life of the individual so that he may truly enter upon the Path of Light.

Chaotic, irrational thinking and feeling, rashness, hostility, anger, arrogance, pride, idealistic day-dreaming, emotional instability, sensitiveness, romantic delusions, lust, depression, suspicion, indecision, sorrow, worry, intoxication, vagueness, bigotry or hate have no place in the life of one who would succeed, one who would truly walk the Path to victory.

At the root of all these things (and their name is truly legion) lies the seed of the delusion of separation.

With the free expression of any separative act, the seed is sown anew and thus binds the individual to the wheel of birth and death. The "crop" must be "harvested" — the consequences of our actions must be experienced and it is only in incarnate existence that this can be done.

The value of being incarnate becomes evident as the Law of Unity is comprehended. It is only in incarnate existence that one is able to "burn the tares" — account for those actions which have proven to be harmful to the growth of the soul. The task of ordering one's thoughts, words, actions and making an objective assessment of one's true status in life must be undertaken. Until this done, there is no way to see which areas of the individual's life need correcting.

One cannot afford to be torn between conflicting thoughts and troubled emotions. These states must be equilibrated so that the cause of a particular experience can be dealt with and either neutralized or sublimated and thus give way to a new expression which incorporates images, thoughts and feelings based on a comprehension of the Law of Unity.

The personality-being is limited to intellectualizing, emotionalizing and reacting, however it can present the appearance of being something more. Yet it is only an appearance. The personality-being will always seek some separative, selfish, personally-gratifying goal. There is no substitute for doing the Great Work — as neither reading about it will do , nor simply thinking or wishing will accomplish it.

One must get to work, arrange and order

all personal matters so that one first learns to become master of one's own time. There is no sense in attempting the work if one is still "a victim of circumstance."

A clear, sober assessment of the inner thoughts, feelings, desires and actions, must be accomplished. There must be a thorough examination yet extremism is to be avoided at all times. Balance is the key. Until one knows what it is that needs correction, as well as what aid is available to help accomplish the task, one has not considered the cost. Through the Great Work the personality is changed. And one needs to know what will be changed so as to properly prepare oneself. What is the cost?

Far from what most will imagine, what is required of one that he may begin the Great Work is really nothing more than giving up entirely any sense of personal autonomy for any thought, word or act. This is the price. Arranging one's daily affairs allows one to plan specific periods for specific actions designed to accelerate the elimination of those aspects and expressions that are representative of separatism as well as implementing the incorporation of those processes which will allow the restructuring of the personality.

The old personality-being cannot travel the Path of Light. Only the personality which has been built according to the Law of Unity can develop the vision to withstand the brilliance of the Light. Images created in the Light of Life express true vision and comprehension of the Life-process. This vision enables one to eliminate those expressions which have proven to be unbalanced and replace them with ones which affirm the Law of Unity. It is in this posture that one is able to walk the Path of Light.

CORPUS CHRISTI / 19

LIBERTY OF THE GOSPELS
REGENERATIO

All Knowledge is within the Universal Mind. This Knowledge can and may be utilized for the benefit of all. Unfortunately there are relatively few who know how to and do access this fount of All-knowledge. Thus Man walks in delusion and snare and is bound to a non-regenerative life-style of self-seeking and ignorance.

If an individual completes the necessary preliminary work and consciously decides to enter the Path of Light
— having arranged and ordered both his time and affairs in order to maintain the chosen course, eliminating those expressions which are seen as a hindrance — that individual becomes eligible for inner instruction as to the practices necessary to accomplish the Great Work.

A consequence of engaging in the preliminary work is that the individual comes to a profound realization of the true degree of his ignorance. Until this realization is experienced, one cannot hear the Voice of the Christ Hierophant. Not until one is ready to surrender all cherished and treasured bits of false knowledge as well as all wishes and desires of greatness and fortune — completely abandoning them for the Light — can that individual begin to be instructed interiorly.

The Spiritual School of Light is not, as some might imagine, an organization engaged solely in secret rituals and meetings, exacting strict and extreme obligations of loyalty and secrecy — although it has been necessary for many of the School's outer vehicles to implement some of these rigid requirements depending on the time period in which the particular expression of the School was functioning. The Inner Spiritual School has existed for the benefit of Man since the beginning of this present expression of the Divine Life-cycle.

Preparation to be instructed by the Christ Hierophant involves a complete surrender of any ideas that the candidate is going to be able to escape life! To the contrary, what is required is more active involvement in life.

The individual must adopt an attitude of complete ignorance as to anything dealing with the true Spiritual Reality as well as develop an intense willingness to abandon any cherished notions concerning spiritual matters. It is with this attitude that one begins to develop a childlike wonder and eagerly awaits the instruction of the Christ Hierophant.

Through a reasoned and objective approach one must find and enter in at the straight gate. For each person this will vary, but each must find the straight gate for himself. It requires an accurate and objective assessment of one's role in life — a comprehension of the True Purpose, and the ability to eliminate thoughts and actions which are now seen as disruptive or unbalanced.

The keen perception of what needs to be eliminated can indicate that the individual has begun to receive the preliminary instructions on self-regeneration from the Christ Hierophant of the Spiritual School of Light.

Much has been written concerning the idea of Regeneration and unfortunately, much of what has been written is nonsense. The Wise have never given specific instructions concerning the Art of Regeneration because they know it cannot be written down. It will be stated however, that without any question, the term regeneration as used in this lesson has nothing at all to do with any abnormal restrictions or perverted expressions of the sex function. To the pure all things are pure; there is only one God.

Our sense of self, as an individual, may be compared to a single ray of a central light source. Each ray brings to light a particular and unique aspect of the central light. Any sense of a separate self that is experienced is due to the inherent quality of the Parent light source to be aware of itself — and this is common to each ray. Yet — singularly and independently — a ray has no real "self" of its own.

This inherent awareness manifesting in each ray may be likened somewhat to a lens, with this 'lens' possessing certain abilities and/or functions. When the lens is operational and focused, the light from the Parent source shines through uninhibited. When the lens is dysfunctional or clouded, the flow of light from the source is restricted.

The idea of 'bringing the lens into focus' involves

a complete reversal in thinking as regards the Parent source of light, because the lens — the inherent quality of self-awareness — can and does present the illusion of being the Parent source within the ray.

To the extent this illusion is accepted as reality, all images remain clouded by the delusion the illusion breeds. A regenerated personality-being may be compared to a clean, clear, focused lens. The Great Work may be compared to removing the impurities from the lens. Receiving instruction as to the means of cleaning the lens requires a complete and total surrender to the influx of the true Parent Source of Light, which is not confined to the limits of the single ray. This brings to mind the words of the Christ Hierophant, "When thine eye is single, thy whole body shall be full of light."

Becoming receptive to the Parent Source of Light requires that the delusion of personal power be destroyed. The sense of self inherent in the Light but confined by the ray, must be freed or released from the confines of the ray. The old lens must be replaced and a new sense of self — a new lens — must be established as being seated at the center of the Parent Source. In this way, one must be "twice born." Thus, the Christ Hierophant advised, "Unless a man be born from above, he cannot see the Kingdom of God." Until our sense of identity is joined to the One Light, we cannot behold the vision of our true beauty and glory that is our Divine birthright.

The School of Light stands ever ready to instruct one in the ways of spiritual life and regeneration, with instruction that brings a complete reversal in the thinking of the pupil. This reversal is accomplished as a pupil practices the fundamentals of spiritual life based upon the Law of Unity. We are joined to all of life. The result of this reversal is the awakening of the knowledge and awareness of the Parent Source of Light within the pupil. As knowledge and awareness of the Light increase, the sense of personal will and separate identity decreases, until finally it is gone. One is then "born of water and of air (spirit) and has direct vision and perception of the kingdom of God."

SANCTUS / 20

THE GLORY OF GOD
REALIZATION

There is sufficient scientific data to prove the powers and list the uses of sound as an actual force. It is suggested that the reader become familiar with this information if at all possible. This writing does not deal with that aspect of the power of sound. We use sound to communicate our thoughts and feelings via speech and there are other ways sound is utilized to accomplish certain tasks, and much is being done in the laboratories of science to develop them.

The example of the vocalist shattering a crystal glass may be cliché, but it illustrates quite clearly that sound is a real force and it has uses other than communicating an idea from one person, place or thing to another. There are sounds that exist which communicate ideas reflecting a larger perception of reality. Needless to say, there are also sounds reflecting a distorted view of reality that can be heard. There is a real need to be able to discern the difference.

We use articulate sound to convey or express an idea, thought or emotion. This sound is always accompanied by a mental image in sympathy with the sound much like the pattern that is formed by grains of sand when a tuning fork is placed near the sand.

The action of the vocalist shattering a glass

is indicative of sound being a natural force with destructive capabilities, and while the example of grains of sand on a dish rearranging themselves under the influence of vibrations from a tuning fork displays sound as a formative power.

Any attempt at transmutation of the personality requires the destruction of the false sense of identity with the lower self or biological man. Any belief in the separate, personal autonomy of the biological personality must be totally dissolved. The idea being — that the death of the separative consciousness brings life to the awakening spiritual being.

After proper preparation it is possible to begin receiving an influx of Light substance that affects a certain center in the subtle vehicles as well as the physical vehicle, much in the same manner as the examples of the vocalist's affecting the glass and the tuning fork's influencing the sand.

This center maybe thought of as a special type of receiver. Communication with the Light can only be achieved through this center, as the subtle nature of the sound transmitted requires a specially tuned "receiver."

Receptivity to this Light substance makes it possible to be instructed interiorly on all subjects necessary for the transmutation of the personality to progress. The Light enables one to discern the operation of a True Identity as it functions through the personality, an awareness of life develops based on the reality of this true identity and not the personality.

Perseverance in being receptive to the Light, will result in a state where a continual flow of knowledge and information which is outside the bounds of the normal time-space reference begins. This instruction is perceived as being perpetual because there is no time in which it is not forthcoming.

The instruction leads to a distinct relationship with the Light that causes an alteration in the entire being, an alteration that affects the subtle vehicles in their interaction and activity in such a way that a new 'sensorium' develops in the individual and an awareness of a new field of Life dawns. An entirely new zodiac is formed and the influence of a new microcosmic constellation manifests in him/her.

We realize that True Life is eternal and as aspects of that One Life, there cannot be a death in any real sense for us. Change is the constant. Death, once a dread enemy, is now seen as a necessary and beneficent process in this earthly life. We are aware that the True Identity of all of Humanity is one and the same. "In Him we live, move and have our being."

There are sounds that exist which communicate ideas reflecting a larger perception of reality. Needless to say, there are also sounds reflecting a distorted view of reality that can be heard. There is a real need to be able to discern the difference.

The creation story in Genesis declares "And The Elohim said Let There Be Light. And there was Light." and the Gospel of John begins with "In the beginning was the Word...... and the Word was God..." Sound and light vibrations are the basis and foundation of all creation. Everything in existence has a unique vibratory status. Variations in the range, frequency and intensity of this vibratory status determine the nature and character of the creation or creature. The degree of variation reveals the intelligence empowering the vibration. The candidate of the Mysteries is faced with the task of discovering just who and what it is that defines his present existence.

Sound, light, vibration, creativity and intelligence — all indissolubly linked, all connected in a way — that needs to be understood and recognized. In the symbolism of the Ageless Wisdom there is a picture of a being (or creature of a different life-wave) blowing a trumpet/horn and below this being three people are shown rising from coffins and reacting to the sound of the horn. In some religions this image is thought of as symbolizing the event known as Judgment Day.

After proper preparation it is possible to begin receiving an influx of Light subslance that affects a certain center in the subtle vehicles as well as the physical vehicle, much in the same manner as the examples of the vocalist affecting the glass and the tuning fork influencing the sand.

The three people in the picture are standing in their coffins in three distinct postures. The man is expressing a devotional attitude in his response to the sound of the horn and the woman is in a stance displaying complete adoration. The child in the middle shows open and direct receptivity to the sound. There is a cloud separating the people from the being who blows the horn.

Our three-dimensional consciousness is being influenced by all sorts of 'vibratory intelligence' of one nature or another. The purpose of the majority of these influences is to keep the consciousness focused on the three-dimensional existence. A focus which keeps one bound to the material and imprisons the individual in a three-dimensional reality. Any true hope of being freed from the confines of this — any real promise of help — must be found in the realization of a reality of a higher and different vibration.

Three-dimensional thinking — the illusion that there is such a thing as time — is what imprisons the individual. Realization of a higher and different reality — the perception of perpetuity of consciousness — is what liberates the individual from the coffins of three-dimensional thinking.

Sound, light, vibration, creativity and intelligence — all indissolubly linked, all connected — compile a true science based on these principles and which is used by all emissaries of the Light to accomplish their task. This is a science that speaks of true knowledge and wisdom and that reveals the true nature of the Light.

VICTORY / 7

THE GREATEST OF THESE
THE ONE WHO OVERCOMES

Realization of the Law of Unity and of the continuity of consciousness brings at the same time an ability to be aware of a separation from certain aspects of the life expression as well as particular levels of consciousness. This is a paradox.

In the old Mystery Schools, the riddle of the Sphinx was used to help the Neophyte understand this very profound teaching concerning the Law of Unity and the continuity of consciousness. The answer to the sphinx's riddle — "Man", brings to mind the saying "Man, know thyself." This knowledge is gained through the death of the false sense of self shared by most of Humankind.

The strange creature mentioned by the sphinx that walked on four — then two — then three legs is meant to represent the personality-being passing through the cycles of birth, growth and decline. The true Mystery Schools of all ages have the knowledge and teach the method of how to be free from this seemingly endless cycle. Solving the riddle of the sphinx is the key to discovering the way to liberation.

The sense of personal autonomy is an illusion created by the One Creative Power. It serves as a tool for the Central Identity to experience the variety of its own unity. What is subject to the endless cycles of birth, growth, decline and death is the personality-being complex and all of the associated vehicles of expression — physical, astral, emotional and mental.

The personality-being is not a microcosm, the microcosm in this world is the living consciousness whose physical body is the sun. It in turn is one of the many reflections of the inner identity of the True Self whose physical body is manifest creation, all of Cosmos.

What an individual may experience as a sense of separate identity is but a reflection of the inner identity of the particular solar microcosm to which one belongs. In light of this, any question as to whether or not life on other worlds exists is answered. There are as many expressions and forms of life as there are images of the true self potential possessed by any microcosm. We, human beings, are reflections of the microcosm's image of itself as being one with the Universal Identity.

The microcosm of our life cycle as Human beings is the consciousness personified and symbolized in the writings and life of the Christ. The Universal Christ is the consciousness of all Cosmos, working according to the Law of Unity. To the degree that the individual is brought into alignment with the Microcosm that manifested as the Christ, to that same degree that individual partakes of and reflects this Microcosm's sense of unity with the Universal One, which is Eternal Life Itself manifesting.

To be receptive to this influx of Light, Life and Knowledge of the Universal Self is the goal of all occultists, mystics, gnostics, alchemists, etc. The key to obtaining this goal lies in the ability of the individual to grasp the true nature of Man. Thus the saying, "Man, know thyself."

Unless one is consciously aligned with the Central Identity of all Life — sees his place in the scheme of things, wherein he has dominion — he will be devoured by the monstrosity of delusion and unbalanced force which is the animal nature of the untransmuted personality-being. Thus when the Christ Hierophant said His body was the Bread of Life, He spoke sublime spiritual truth. For to eat of this Bread is to hunger no more.

We are sustained and nourished through our conscious alignment with the influx of Light, Life and Knowledge flowing from the Solar Microcosm, which is in direct union with the consciousness of Cosmos, the Universal Self. In one Rosicrucian writing, the central figure, a "Brother C. R. C." whose body was said to have been found in a vault, had several inscriptions around his pastos. Yet the most prominent inscription read, "Jesus is my All". Instruction from the inner Spiritual School of Light brings new insight regarding this statement.

Receptivity to the guidance of the Christ Hierophant totally destroys the existing personality complex and regenerates a completely new vehicle of expression which is truly a temple of the Living God, eternal in the Heavens, not made with hands. This regenerated personality serves as a perfect tool for the Solar Microcosm to complete Its particular work and purpose in this present life-cycle.

The Solar Microcosm, working through a

regenerated personality, manifests as an individual who has dominion in his life due to his identification with the source of all dominion. Thus Jesus was able to perform miracles and control the elements of this world because he was in conscious union with the original Creative Consciousness operating behind the veil of manifest creation, i.e., the Father in Heaven.

The path to Victory and the key to our release from bondage rests on our ability to receive true inner instruction from the Christ Hierophant. Via this instruction our personalities are transmuted so that they serve as perfected vehicles of the Central Self, that Self which has dominion over all the elements of manifestation and is therefore free from the bonds of separative thinking.

The individual consciously united to the Solar Microcosm expresses as a personality quite the contrary to most of Humanity. The most notable characteristic is a genuine love for Humanity which is spawned from a direct knowledge of the unity of life. There is control exerted over the nature kingdom that appears miraculous to the ignorant. The individual expresses a temperament of true magnanimity and beneficence.

By the Will of Divine Omnipotence, Man was given dominion over the works of God. The individual who has, through the guidance and instruction of the inner Spiritual School of Light, entered the Path of Light and has become joined to the consciousness of the Solar Microcosm (become a member of the Body of Christ), directs the forces and kingdoms of life as a direct and conscious mediator for Divinity Itself, becoming truly a house of the Living God.

The way to Victory requires work. When all traces of separative thinking are eliminated from the mind of the individual — when one has reasoned the true order of the creative process, and is willing to sacrifice all sense of personal autonomy, to incorporate the Law of Unity as the foundation of all knowledge, then can one begin to partake of the Bread of Life, the Body of Christ.

THE ORACLE / 5

REVELATION

"Blessed is he that readeth, and they that hear the words of this prophecy, and keep those things which are written therein; for the time is at hand.... to the seven churches which are in Assiah; Grace be unto you, and peace, from Him which is, and which was, and which is to come; and from the seven Spirits which are before his throne."

The Book of Revelation is a most cryptic and therefore misunderstood writing in the Bible. In this rather cryptic — yet vivid account is hidden a key to the Great Work. In any attempt to explore the mystery of the Revelation of St. John, the Magical Language must be considered.

The quotation above has phrases expressed in the syntax of the Magical Language. Please note the spelling in regard to the word Assiah and contrast it with the text rendering of Asia. This is a first clue as to which realm is being discussed in this work. The Great Work takes place on the physical plane not in some far-off netherworld. This quotation tells the instructed that the process involved is that of the alignment and transmutation of the seven vehicles and the uninhibited expression of the higher intelligent energy through them.

The number seven is very significant in the Mysteries and its symbolism has been employed by all the various outer vehicles of the one true Inner School. The ancient Alchemist recognized seven metals as being involved in the transmutation process; the original Astrologers considered seven planets as being the forces governing human behavior. In the Hermetic writings the Principles of Truth are listed as being seven in number. In the old Qabalistic cipher known as the Sepher Yetzirah, or Book of Formation, the seven double letters of the Magical Language are discussed. It admonishes the reader to be aware that seven is the significant number: "The double letters are seven, and not six, they are seven and not eight; reflect upon this fact, inquire into it, realize its importance, so that the Creator may return to His Throne." From the Eastern teachings, comes the concept of the seven chakras or Holy centers in the body.

All of these examples are really speaking of the same thing from various vantage points; the same is true of the writings in Revelation. The basic make-up of human personality is much more than might be imagined on casual consideration. The One Identity maintains and operates through each human personality in such a way that in the world of Assiah, each individual has seven bodies or vehicles. In each of these bodies the One Intelligence operates at a different level of vibration and awareness. The outer-most body, our physical vehicle, vibrates at the slowest rate and is the least aware of the true spiritual force that is its source of origin. The innermost body — our true, real vehicle vibrates at the fastest rate and is in full awareness of the One Light that is living each individual personality.

It is an accepted fact in science and physics in particular, that when light strikes a triangular prism, seven distinct rays of color manifest. In a similar fashion, the one Light is expressed in a sevenfold manner through each individual. When there is a flaw in a prism, it will distort and bend the rays in such a manner that some colors will predominate, others will diminish by being absorbed and there will be an asymmetrical distribution of the light. The untransmuted personality-being is like a prism with flaws. It distorts and misrepresents the intent of the One Light's attempting to shine through. The Great Work involves the restoration of the "prism" so to speak, in order that the One Light may express uninhibited through an individual.

    The seven Churches in Assiah are the seven vehicles of each individual. In the physical body there are seven nerve centers that correspond to the seven vehicles and through which all seven vehicles interact and have influence upon the personality expression. These nerve centers are not the vehicles, they are all within the physical body. Each of the seven vehicles is a complex and distinct "body" in itself and has seven "centers" of interaction with the other vehicles. Each of the seven centers in each of the seven vehicles is the point of contact with the One Light for every individual. The Angels of the Churches represent the sevenfold Spirit as it operates through and utilizes the seven vehicles.

    The Grace spoken of in the quotation is another term whose meaning is revealed through consideration of the Magical Language. In the tradition of the Qabalah, the word "Grace" is a shorthand notation for the term "Secret Wisdom" and it refers to the fact that the way to balance and align the seven vehicles is a great secret to most of humanity.

NESHEMAH / 21

DOMINION

"These things saith He that holdeth the seven stars in His right hand, who walketh in the midst of the seven golden candlesticks: ... To the Victor will I give to eat of the Tree of Life."

This passage is the first of seven that deal with the activity of the Sacred Fire in the seven Holy Centers of the individual as well as their proper functioning.

The Tree of Life is central to the mysteries of the Holy Qabalah and much has been written in the current times concerning the Tree. It is important to understand that the Tree of Life refers to the true structure of your real spiritual body. There are several good books written on the subject all of which contain a diagram representing this Tree. It is a diagram showing ten circles in a certain geometric relationship with lines or "paths" connecting the ten circles. As with all symbols there is the danger of mistaking the symbol for the idea or principle it is intended to represent. It is important for one to remember that the true Tree of Life is his/her spiritual vehicle, fully functional, in proper alignment and proper relationship with all of its counterparts. As a symbol, the Tree of Life is a glyph or map of Divine Consciousness, detailing Its activity within the framework of Humanity.

The "Church" of Ephesus is the center that has its physical correlate in the body in the area at the base of the spine. This center contains a very concentrated and extremely potent energy vibration which in most adults is in a state of limited functioning. To release the energy of this center without proper preparation is to cause certain and unalterable damage to the psyche of the individual. When the Ephesus center is properly awakened and the force operates in a balanced manner, it produces in the individual what is called "cosmic consciousness."

When an individual incarnates, the Ephesus center is the center that holds and stores the memory of all the works of that individual through all of his incarnations. It is in this center that the degree of one's immersion in materiality is marked. The more materialistic and "earth-bound" an individual is, the greater is the restriction of the flow of the energy from this center. Thus it takes lifetimes for some to achieve the uninhibited flow of the Ephesus energy. Individuals who are in a rush to experience cosmic consciousness or Nirvana as it is called in the eastern philosophy, seldom make much progress and actually may even further limit the flow of this center's energy with their impatience.

The energy of the Ephesus center vibrates in a dual fashion. One might visualize it as spiraling clockwise and counter-clockwise at the same time. The spinal cord is the "channel" through which the energy flows. The Ephesus center connects the individual with the true Spiritual Kingdom — with the Christ. When its operation is restricted, one is a slave to this world and the things of this world. When the Ephesus center is operating in harmony with the Christ, one has dominion over this world and the things of this world.

The Will of the Christ is that we return to our "first

love," His Kingdom. This requires that one repudiate all that is material and earthly, seeking only that which is of Christ's Kingdom. To describe the Heavenly Kingdom in words is not possible. One cannot describe in words that which is not of this world. The Great Work aims at helping the individual to place his mind into a proper, receptive state in order to directly perceive the inner Kingdom through the Grace of God. This takes patience and hard work, but it is work that is gladly undertaken when one realizes the benefit that will result from such efforts.

GRACE / 16

GRACE

"These things saith the First and the Last, which was dead, and is alive ... the Victor shall not be hurt of the second death."

This passage in Revelation deals with a subject that can be very disturbing to the average person — the idea of a second death. The questions asked most frequently concerning this subject are, "How is it possible to die twice? — Is not physical death final and complete?" The answer of course is "no," that physical death is only the first of a twofold process, a process wherein the One Self of each individual withdraws its focused attention first from the physical plane and second from the astral plane.

Our sense of time is an artificial one and is based solely upon the illusion produced by the phenomena of the physical plane. The astral plane is in a sense a reflection in reverse and in some ways a caricature of the physical plane; perhaps it would be more accurate to say that the physical plane is a caricature of the astral plane. In any event, it is difficult to develop a sense of time as it truly relates to the astral plane using physical plane examples. Nonetheless, time on the astral plane may be conceived of as occurring in cycles, tides or periods, much like the activity of the moon. Considered from earth standards, the moon waxes and wanes, is visible completely (full), in sections (first quarter, last quarter), or is not visible at all (new). At the times when it is not visible at all, it could be said that it was "empty" just as when it is completely visible it is said to be full.

The astral plane also has phases when it is full, when it is empty, when it is between these two states or where it is either becoming fuller or more empty. This happens on a cosmic level as well as on an individual level. At this stage in our life-cycle, the astral is full and heading toward the last quarter (emptying) . Each individual faces this process when his consciousness is withdrawn from the physical plane. For a time there is a sense of being in a new land and a new environment; one is able to see just how the physical plane was and is indeed a temporary residence. Then a new process takes place, one similar to that on the physical plane, where the individual has to learn about his new surroundings and his new status in the community. Likewise on the physical plane, there are teachers and other forms of assistance to aid the individual in acquiring the necessary information.

The information gathered on the astral plane has a more profound significance than most of the learning that is done on the physical plane because what is to be discovered on the astral is just how much or, as in most cases, how little soul-growth has taken place during the brief stay on earth. This period of learning on the astral may be compared to the waxing of the moon, of the full cycle. When all that can be learned is learned — the individual realizes to what extent work still needs to be done and also in what areas progress has been made — the "moon is full," so to speak.

What follows next is that the individual is faced with several decisions and depending on how much progress the individual has made, the decisions are either painful and distressing or they are joyful and liberating. It is in this cycle that the emptying takes place. All errors must be reconciled (emptied) and only that which is of soul value is retained. It is in the "waning" cycle that the decisions concerning the next incarnation on the physical plane take place, i.e., decisions about where to incarnate, into what type of family situation to incarnate, with what racial type, what gender, what socioeconomic standing and health status, et cetera. All of this is determined by just what it is that the soul has decided is most important to help correct the errors made during the previous incarnation.

These decisions determine what type of personality the individual will have long before the individual is born into the physical world. Finally, with the lessons learned and decisions made, the "moon wanes" and all sense of personality that was developed in the former life is emptied. This ending is what is referred to as the second death.

To be free from the second death is to have developed a personality that is totally receptive to the influence of the Christ Hierophant. To develop such a personality, one must have the energy of the Smyrna center completely balanced and properly functioning. It is important to be reminded that in our discussions of the seven centers we are not to focus intentionally on physical correlates. The area of the body that corresponds to the Smyrna center is the prostatic ganglion, located just below the navel. It is the area of the nervous system that controls the reproductive functions.

It is the energy of the Smyrna center that gives the individual a sense of personal volition and a sense of separate identity. The energy of this center is closely related to the elemental fire. Most of the separative acts of selfishness and cruelty can be directly related to the unbalanced operation of the energy of the Smyrna center. When the Smyrna energy expresses through an individual in a negative fashion, the actions of that individual are considered sinful. One has only to consider the area of the physical body which is attributed to the Smyrna center to see the connection. From the beginning, the use of the reproductive energy has been associated with the original sin. This is due largely to a misunderstanding and misinterpretation of Genesis. It is only when the Smyrna energy is unbalanced that so-called sin occurs.

Sin, in truth, is a missing of the mark. It is failure to express the Smyrna energy in a positive, balanced manner. The misuse of the Smyrna energy, especially in terms of the reproductive function, leads to the retardation of soul-growth and the accumulation of much unwanted experience-data that must be "emptied" when the individual is on the astral plane. Acts of overt cruelty and tyranny are also examples of the negative expression of the Smyrna energy. Any display of selfishness and personal gratification at the expense of others indicates the negative expression of this energy.

As long as the Smyrna energy is unbalanced, it will not interact with the other centers properly and will actually cause the other centers to malfunction. When the seven centers cannot function harmoniously, chaos is the result. This affects the personality in such a way that the individual engages in activities that are harmful to him, resulting in the withdrawal of the focus of the Higher Genius or death.

Until contact with the Christ Hierophant is made, the Smyrna energy will function in an unbalanced manner. It is only by a matter of degree that some people have a more positive output of this energy than others. It is only with the help and instruction of the Christ Hierophant that one is able to balance this energy and express it in such a manner that affirms the truth of the Law of Unity. It is only through the grace of the Christ Hierophant that we are able to restore the Smyrna energy, become receptive to the influence of Divine Will and begin to act accordingly.

With the aid of the Christ Hierophant, the individual can set the functioning of the Smyrna center aright and begin to construct a personality that is a monument worthy of housing the presence of God. This is a personality that does not need to be discarded during the "waning of the moon," one that endures and goes on to serve the Creator in ever grander ways and one that is not hurt by the second death.

ARCHITECT / 14

WEALTH

"These things saith He which hath the sharp sword with two edges ... to the Victor will I give to eat of the hidden manna, and I will give him a white stone, and in the stone a new name written, which no man knoweth saving he that receiveth it."

In this present age of technology-culture it would appear that Humankind has reached the pinnacle of knowledge and wisdom. Every day science announces a breakthrough in some field of endeavor or some area of research. Keeping pace with all these advances in science, there is an ever increasing clamor for knowledge that science has as yet been unable to satisfy — the area dealing with knowledge of the Self.

It seems as if each day there is a new organization or movement appearing on the scene claiming to have the answer to the age-old questions which have been asked since the beginning of recorded history, i.e., "What is Man? Why is Man? Where is Man's place in the scheme of life?" Yet with all of Humankind's riches in material possessions and information, there is still vast poverty when it comes to Self-knowledge and spiritual awareness.

Much of what is passing for a "new" teaching or method is really the revival of ancient superstitions and foolishness which are to a great extent responsible for Humankind's current state of ignorance regarding spiritual matters. Some "new" practices are in truth, the repackaging of some old and quite dangerous methods which lead to unbalanced psychic development. The Preacher spoke wisely when he said, "there is no new thing under the sun." Life is a cyclic process; all things return to their source. To be certain, the affairs of this world hold no mystery for the enlightened, for those who have partaken of the true Secret Wisdom, the hidden manna.

Stored in the memory of each individual is the record of all past lives and actions. This memory is the key to each individual's life here on earth and on the astral as well. When an individual incarnates, this memory is blocked and the average person has no idea that such a thing even exists. This is necessary because free access to this record of past events would interfere with the individual's ability to deal with the present incarnation. When an individual has made contact with the Christ Hierophant and has reached a certain level of development, he not only recalls memories of his past lives, but he is also given access to the Cosmic Memory wherein are stored the records of entire Life-cycles.

Comprehension of the cyclic process of creation is possible, but in order to be able to grasp the workings of the-Life-Power, one must be receptive to the Universal Memory wherein is stored the record of all events past, present and future. Creation exists because of this Memory. All the prophets and sages of past times were able to tune into this Cosmic Memory and thus were able to guide and direct their followers when they had strayed too far from the indicated path. The average, unenlightened individual has no access to this Memory because he/she has not yet reached a stage of development where such access is warranted.

There are many who seek information about a past life or incarnation. Any attempts to force recall of past lives is not recommended. Most want to believe that they were kings and queens and other sorts of royalty in former lives. The truth of the matter is far less grandiose; an individual's present life is a direct and clear indication of what all other lives have been, for we are the sum total of all of them.

It is an act of Divine Mercy that the record of past lives and events is blocked from the average individual's memory, for it prevents foolish attempts to correct what has already been done. It also stops one from keeping his attention focused on the past instead of the present. When an individual is truly dedicated to living this present life in harmony with the laws that govern creation, then access is granted to the wisdom and knowledge stored in the Cosmic Memory which is necessary to fulfill the work of this present life.

The Pergamos center corresponds to the physical nerve center known as the solar plexus located just above the navel. It is not to be confused with the "sun" center although its name would seem to indicate a connection. It is through this center that we gain access to the Cosmic Memory. The energy of this center, when operating in a balanced fashion, gives the individual a true sense of the operations of Spirit and of the orderly, cyclic processes that make up the Universe. It is the energy center that gives an individual the sense of being connected to a greater whole and counteracts the influence of the earth plane vibration. Through the Pergamos center one makes contact with the Spiritual Hierarchy and communes with all other individuals who are on the same Path. It is through the Pergamos center that one realizes the vastness of Cosmos and the true immensity of the Universal Mind.

When the Pergamos center is functioning in a balanced manner, the Christ Hierophant can begin the work of instructing the individual in the ways of preparation for being ordained into the ministry of the order of Melchizedek. This is a high privilege and the ordination is not complete until all the centers have been brought into balanced operation. However, the preparation begins with this center. When the Pergamos center is activated, the Christ Hierophant indicates to the individual the steps necessary to become a citizen in the New City of Jerusalem. It is at this stage that the Christ Hierophant indicates to the individual what his life in the Kingdom shall be and what his duties and responsibilities are to be. The balanced, activated operation of the Pergamos center gives the individual a new sense of being, a sense of being a universal entity and not just an earth-bound mortal.

FOHAT / 8

FERTILITY

"These things saith the Son of God, who hath His eyes like unto a flame of fire, and His feet are like fine brass ... to the Victor will I give power over the nations."

Think of the Thyatira Center as the center that functions as a mediator between the three lower centers and the three above it. The preceding centers in one way or another all deal with the lower self, the personality-being level of our consciousness. The remaining four centers are all involved with the workings of the Higher Being as well as the energy that comprises our individual being.

In our solar system there are planets with their respective satellites — moons, asteroids, meteors, et cetera. Although many of the planets are far from our planet earth and others are relatively close, science has been able to determine that the activities of all the planets as well as their satellites, are influenced by the sun. In fact all the planets are in orbit around the sun and draw their "life" from the energy of the sun. Each planet also has its own individual characteristics and features that distinguish it from the other planets, yet all their individual qualities depend upon the relationship of each of them to the sun — their distance from the sun, the number of times they revolve around the sun and the manner in which they revolve around the sun. All these affect each planet, determining the way each planet functions in relation to the other planets as well as individually.

The sun is the controlling factor and it has its cycles as well, moving within a greater system called our galaxy. Within the scheme of the galaxy, the sun is in motion making its own revolutions through the various groups of constellations and in so doing it exposes all of the planets to the influences of the various regions of the galaxy. As the sun moves through its cycle it interacts with the energy of the Cosmos and because the planets are all moving with the sun, they are influenced by the energies as well.

The Thyatira center — similar to the sun, is the center that influences the other six centers and determines the quality of their operation. Just as the planets would be cold, lifeless bodies drifting in space without the light and heat of the sun, the inner centers would be vortices of blind, unintelligent force without the conscious, sentient energy of the Thyatira center. It is the Thyatira center energy that brings the influence of the intelligence of the Higher Mind into the consciousness of the individual and is what gives each person a sense of individual identity. It is the Thyatira center that is responsible for the "I" consciousness we all experience. The balanced functioning and operation of each of the other centers is determined by the energy output of the Thyatira center.

The Thyatira center corresponds to the cardiac ganglion in the body located near the heart. In the Western mysteries this center has been called the heart center. This is a fitting description of the Thyatira center because in order to express the energy of this center in a proper fashion, it 'takes heart' so to speak. This is the center that is the transmitting / receiving station for the Love of the Christ. When this energy is not expressing in a balanced manner it can express in ways that are self centered, egotistical, "cold-hearted," vain, and show a total disregard for any other individual. When an individual is not open to the influence of the Christ Hierophant, it is the energy of the Thyatira center that is affected. Fear is the stumbling block. It is through the Thyatira center that we receive our sense of individuality, it is also through this center that we must surrender in order to partake of the influence of the One Identity centered in the Higher Being of the Christ Hierophant.

To control the operations of the other centers is to become one with the energy of the Thyatira center. The key to uniting with this energy is to open the heart to the love of Christ. Just as the rays of the sun warm all of the planets keeping each one vital in its own respect, the love of the Christ Hierophant radiating through the Thyatira center, energizes the other centers keeping them vital. Just as the force of the sun keeps each planet in its respective orbit, the Thyatira center is the ruling force around which the other centers revolve. Because the Thyatira center is responsible for transmitting the energy of the Christ Hierophant and thereby linking us to the Higher Being, it is the Thyatira center in each individual soul that remains with that individual soul through all the cycles of incarnations.

The sun has its cycles through the galaxy and the Thyatira center has its cycles through the many lives of the soul. In each incarnation the soul attempts to bring the energy of the Thyatira center into full and balanced operation so that the other centers may be energized by it thereby becoming imbued with the influence of the Cosmos. It is only then that an individual may attain to conscious immortality. The Thyatira center is the doorway to immortality and it is the energy of the Christ Hierophant radiating through this center that energizes the other centers so that they function in such a manner as to bring this conscious immortality about. In each incarnation the soul works with a new personality, testing it and tempering it, fashioning it so that it will handle the high-intensity energy of the Thyatira center. Some personalities last longer than others; thus some life cycles are longer than others. When a personality can no longer withstand the tempering process, it is discarded and the work begins anew.

With each new personality all the progress of the previous attempts are carried over. When the soul reaches a stage where it has a personality that can successfully undergo the transformation process and handle the energy of the Thyatira center completely, conscious immortality is achieved. It is then that the individual has full recollection of all previous attempts at mastering the energy of this center along with recollection of the reasons for failure in the past. Attaining conscious immortality is the beginning not the end, for once an individual can control the energy of the Thyatira center the real work begins. The cycles of the Thyatira center continue, however they are experienced by a soul that has a vehicle properly fashioned to travel through the galaxy of the inner realms of the Godhead.

While working with the energy of the Thyatira center it is important to keep in mind that this is the heart center, the Christ center and as such we are subject to experience the affairs of daily existence quite differently than would be expected.

Opening the heart to the love of the Christ Hierophant means something other than most would suspect. It was mentioned that some symptoms of the unbalanced expression of the Thyatira energy manifest as an individual with little or no concern about the welfare of others. However, there is another side to this imbalance. The opposite side of indifference is just as unbalanced. It expresses in those individuals who are outraged at every little seeming injustice done to another and who take offense at every opportunity. They are accurately described as "crusaders," always looking for the chance to "ride off," to challenge some imagined tyrant or to balance the scales of justice in favor of some poor unfortunate individual. Needless to say, this is as unbalanced as is cold, unfeeling indifference.

  The balanced expression of the Thyatira energy manifests in an individual who may seem indifferent at first glance, yet closer inspection will reveal a warm compassionate soul, ablaze with the flame of the Sacred Fire, the fire that does not burn. No gushy emotionalism or maudlin sentimentality will be found emanating from such a person. There is concern and deep caring for all yet this individual does not directly interfere in the lives of others for he has direct knowledge that each soul must make the struggle on his own, that is, each soul must try, fail and try again until at last, success is achieved. Individuals who express the balanced Thyatira energy are always willing and eager to assist, although only when asked. Even then, they merely point out the way and never coerce or try to convince another.

AIMA / 3

WISDOM

"These things saith He that hath the seven Spirits of God and the seven stars ... The Victor shall be clothed in white raiment..."

Discussion of the Sardis center concerns the mystery of the process whereby one may begin to develop the capacity to allow the purification of the desire nature to take place.

Desire operates in every individual's life without exception. There is nothing evil or bad about desire, it is a force whose expression is determined by the quality of the consciousness interacting with it. Unbalanced, fragmented consciousness expresses desire as greed, avarice, jealousy, and lust. There are traces of these expressions in even the most sincere, well-meaning, nice people one meets or knows in everyday life. One must be able to consciously turn greed and avarice into aspiration and dedication to the transfiguristic process, turn jealousy into admiration for all the fortunate ones who have succeeded in the Victory Work and are aiding in the quest and lust into love for the Christ Hierophant who is guiding our feet along the Path to Victory.

The Sardis center energy is the energy that manifests as desire in human personality. Desire involves emotion and thought. The emotion of desire is the expression of want due to a feeling of lack or a need for something. The thoughts involved are with finding a solution to the situation. The interaction of the Sardis energy with human consciousness results in the generation of mental images; these images are shaped by the thoughts that accompany the desire. Mental images that are clear, precise and continuously generated, tend to manifest as an actual physical reality. Control of the Sardis center energy allows the individual to perpetuate only those images which are in harmony with his desire to experience the transfiguration. When one has gained conscious control of the Sardis center one has also learned the secret that opens the door to the Victory Temple. It is with the Sardis center energy that one may enter into the higher realms of the Life Power.

It is unsafe both mentally and physically to attempt to suppress desire. The purification of the desire nature — through the refining of mental images and clarification in the thought process, leads to the transfigured state. When desire expresses through a consciousness suffering from the delusion of separateness, it seeks to possess, to take, to hoard. This is an indication that the negative aspect of the force is in operation. When desire is expressing its positive aspect, it results in a caring, giving disposition, seeking to serve, augment and aid. The key to balanced operation of the Sardis energy is in the practice of unselfish service and Love expressed through acts of kindness and compassion.

Refining of the image-making ability involves a change in attitude regarding the pro-creative act as it deals with human beings and creatures. There is neither anything dirty about the pro-creative act, nor is there anything sinful about it. It is the means whereby the life process is maintained on the physical plane. It is the thought which accompanies the act that describes the way an individual feels about the act and determines the outcome of the interaction between the individuals involved in the pro-creative act. The energy that allows us to create physical bodies is the same energy that will enable us to create the celestial vehicle. It is essential to be able to demonstrate that the use of mental imagery is the key to purifying the desire nature and is the way to transfiguration.

The Sardis center is located in the area of the laryngeal plexus or the throat. Its location is significant because it controls the area where sound is produced. It is the voice that allows us to state our desires so that we may perhaps fulfill them. Thought and emotion are revealed through this center; thoughts are clothed in words and emotion is evidenced by the sound that accompanies the words. Sound has a power of which very few individuals are aware. When an image is held in consciousness it has a certain vibratory rate. The sound a voice makes when articulating an image, is directly related to the vibratory rate of that image.

When a sound is vibrating in exact harmony with its corresponding image, that image will manifest as a physical reality. Do not oversimplify this statement. It takes lifetimes to master this ability yet, one must begin somewhere. The Work is to so adjust one's thinking that the Sardis energy may manifest through sounds which clearly indicate a desire for transfiguration.

SOPHIA / 2

PEACE

"These things saith He that is holy, He that is true, He that hath the key of David... The Victor will I make a pillar in the Temple of my God..."

In the Western Mystery tradition the symbolism of pillars carries a definite phallic implication. Pillars are a symbol of the dual expression of the One Creative Energy. In the ancient initiation ceremonies the candidate was led several times through the mystic pillars as he traveled toward the beckoning Light. Pillars also imply stability and permanence.

What is indicated is that the balanced expression of the reproductive energy is the key to conscious immortality. As with everything in manifestation, this energy has a positive and negative aspect. And according to the Hermetic writings, "everything is dual". These two aspects may also be thought of as being active and passive, fixed and volatile, hot and cold. A symbol that represents this energy in balanced operation is the six-pointed star composed of two interlaced triangles one with the apex up and the other with the apex down. This star may be familiar to some as belonging to a particular faith, however, its use as a symbol by the Inner School predates any association with that particular religious use.

The dual expression of the reproductive energy manifests in the human body as two channels of force, one ascending and the other descending along the spinal column. In most individuals the energy is unbalanced on the side of descending force, thus keeping the reproductive organs over stimulated and strained. The work of Transfiguration involves activating the ascending force so that it may energize and stimulate the brain and open what is called by some the "third eye." The key to success in attempting to direct the ascending force lies in the balanced functioning of the Philadelphia center.

The Philadelphia center is the 'network' center for all of the seven centers. It is responsible for the operation of all of the systems that keep the human body functioning, i.e., the heart, lungs, circulatory system, et cetera. The area in the human body that corresponds to the Philadelphia center is the pituitary body located just above and behind the root of the nose. In physiological terms the Philadelphia center is known as the master gland because of its role as regulator.

The balanced expression of the Philadelphia center leads to the awakening of a sensory faculty that allows the individual to become aware of the life expressions that are hidden from anyone who has not yet developed the ability to perceive them. In some schools of thought this faculty is called the third eye because the individual who has awakened this new sense is truly able to "see" into all of the forces and beings that inhabit the astral plane as well as the higher, inner spiritual plane.

The School of Light makes a distinction about this faculty of the Philadelphia center in that most people think being "psychic" means having this center awakened; this is not what the School of Light intends. Most individuals who consider themselves psychic merely catch glimpses of the astral shimmerings that flicker and fade in the unstable substance of that plane.

The individual who has awakened the sight that accompanies the balanced expression and operation of the Philadelphia center has developed true spiritual insight and is able to see into and beyond the surface of all manifest phenomena. The Philadelphia center conveys true foresight and allows one to look to the future and know with certainty that what is observed is correct. When the Philadelphia center is fully functional it gives the individual the ability to actually see the reality of the Law of Unity which links all opposites together in the bond of perfect peace.

It is this vision that allows us to know with certainty that the One Life is immortal and that we each share in that one Life. This knowledge brings a peace of mind that goes beyond words, it is a peace that allows us to rest our lives upon the sure foundation of Eternal Being.

MAGUS / 1

LIFE

"These things saith the Amen, the faithful and true witness, the beginning of the creation of God — to the Victor will I grant to sit with me in my throne..."

In the vernacular of the Magical Language, the word "throne" refers directly to the Laodiceans center. The full functioning of this center in an incarnate human being is the goal of the practical aspects of the Great Work. The correlation of this Laodiceans center to the physical body is the pineal gland located in the forebrain and its astral counterpart resides approximately 18 inches above the head. To succeed in awakening the Laodiceans center into full operation is to discover the true Philosopher's Stone sought by the ancient Alchemists.

When operating fully, it is the Laodiceans center that allows the individual to penetrate the veil of illusion of the material plane and see the connectedness of all manifest phenomena. When one has succeeded in awakening the Laodiceans center one becomes able to perform the works of consciousness that are ascribed to the true Magician of Light.

This center is responsible for an individual's sense of self-awareness and the ability to focus attention on one specific thing as opposed to another. The ability to make fine distinctions between similar things as well as to see the relationship between seeming opposites, derives from the energy of the Laodiceans center.

Through the Laodiceans center the One Self, the true identity of us all, focuses a portion of Its consciousness into the personality of the individual that we call "I". This sense of "I-ness" does not belong to the personality nor does it even reside within the personality. The Laodiceans center is the point of contact for the individual personality and the One Identity, the Infinite, Living Mind.

The level of energy that emanates toward the Laodiceans center from the One Self is so intense and subtle that only relatively few individuals in any one life time succeed in becoming fully consciously aware of its expression. The Work is to bring all of our Centers into balanced operation and thereby strengthen the astral counter-part of the Laodiceans center to the end that ultimately we experience the Touch of the Infinite.

Do not expect this to happen overnight! The work of Transmutation takes lifetimes in some instances and in others a matter of years is all that is involved. We cannot know what our individual timeframe is, but we can work toward the goal with confidence that we shall succeed. If one is in a hurry to finish, he will fail without a doubt. We must work diligently, patiently, confidently and as if we had all eternity to accomplish our goal. Fear invites failure, whereas confidence breeds success.

The development of the Laodiceans center enables the individual to become a true and transparent channel for the One Infinite Intelligence. This is the center that enables one to bring down into the field of manifest phenomena the intelligence of the Higher Genius. In another respect, when the Laodiceans center is operating properly, the consciousness of the individual is raised to a higher level of awareness and function. The ability to manipulate Light is a power that derives from the energy of this center. The practical application of the theory of the Magic of Light depends upon the balanced expression of this power.

FIRST PROCEDURE

Trigonem Igneum

Do NOT formulate any question(s) when doing any of the preliminary procedures. This will require some effort on your part at first, especially if you have a favorite [trusted] method already. But it is mandatory that you DO NOT formulate any question at this stage. Also, DO NOT choose a significator or a card to represent yourself. Of most importance — DO NOT consider any of the meanings of the cards! Simply lay out the cards as instructed and write down the cards that are in the layout. Be sure to keep an accurate record of all exercises.

Step One: Be still for 3 minutes and to the best of your ability, clear you mind of stressful and distracting thoughts. This is not meditation. The aim is to practice being still and calm for a few minutes.

Step Two: Shuffle the cards 5 times and deal the cards — one at a time — face down into the 4 piles as shown in the illustration.
For the first 7 days use only the cards in pile# 1 in the Triangle. The next 7 days use only the cards from pile# 2 in the Triangle. The following 7 days use only the cards from pile#3 in the Triangle.
The last 7 days use only the cards in pile#4 in the Triangle. Thus completing a 28 day cycle. Take note that piles 1&2 will have 20 cards while piles 3&4 will

have 19.

Step Three: Using the chosen pile, shuffle the cards 9 times. Deal the cards — one at a time — face down into the Triangle as indicated in the illustration.
For the first 7 days deal only one card into each place on the triangle [make a record of the cards] and discard the rest. Note: when using only one card for each place on the triangle deal the cards face up.
The next 7 days deal only two cards into each place on the Triangle. Place the cards face up in the two-card layout as shown.
The following 7 days deal only three cards into each place on the Triangle. Place the cards face up in the three-card layout as shown.
When using two and/or three cards, lay out the cards as indicated in the illustration.
The last 7days deal all the cards — one at a time — face down into the places on the Triangle as shown in the diagram.

     Note: when dealing out all the cards: if piles #1&2 were used the Apex and Left Base of the Triangle will have 7 cards and the Right Base will have 6 cards. If piles #3&4 were used the Apex will only have 7 cards and both Bases will have 6 cards.
During the last 7 days of the cycle:
The first 3 days layout the cards in the Left Base only — as shown.
The next day layout the cards in the Apex only as — shown. The last 3 days layout the cards from the Right Base only — as shown.
Practice the First procedure once a day [preferably in the morning - or the beginning of your day] for one month.

FIRST PROCEDURE

Step One: Shuffle the cards 5 times. Deal the cards — one at a time — face down into the four piles in the direction shown. Start at pile #1.

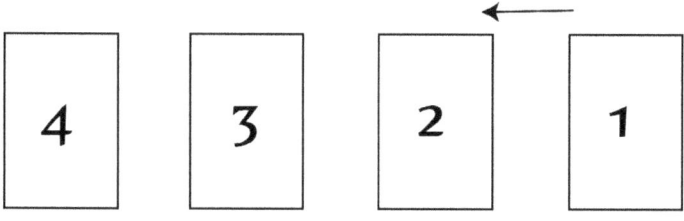

Start Here

Step Two: Using the chosen pile, shuffle the cards 9 times. Deal the cards — one at a time — face down into the Triangle in the direction shown. Start at pile A.

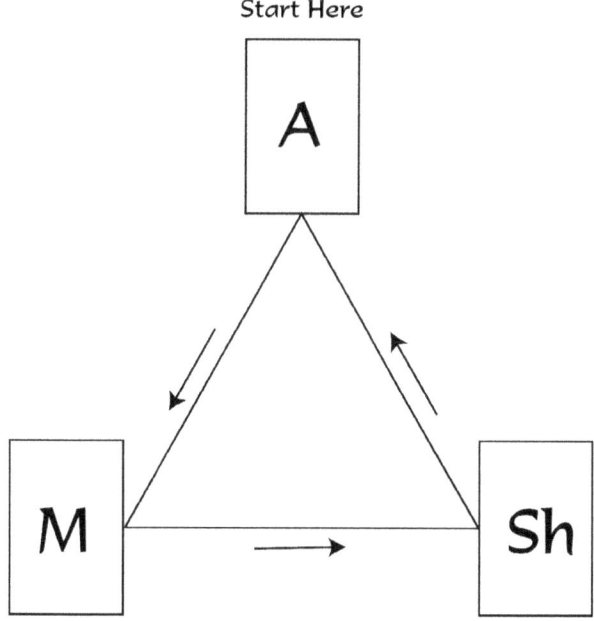

Note: when using only one card for each place on the triangle deal the cards face up.

FIRST PROCEDURE
Two-card Layout.

Start Here

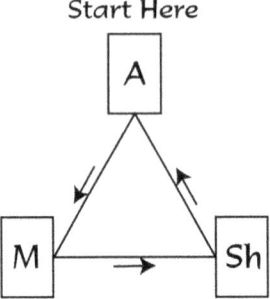

1. Deal two cards — one at a time — face down into each place on the Triangle and discard the remainder.
2. Place the cards face up in the two-card layout as shown below.

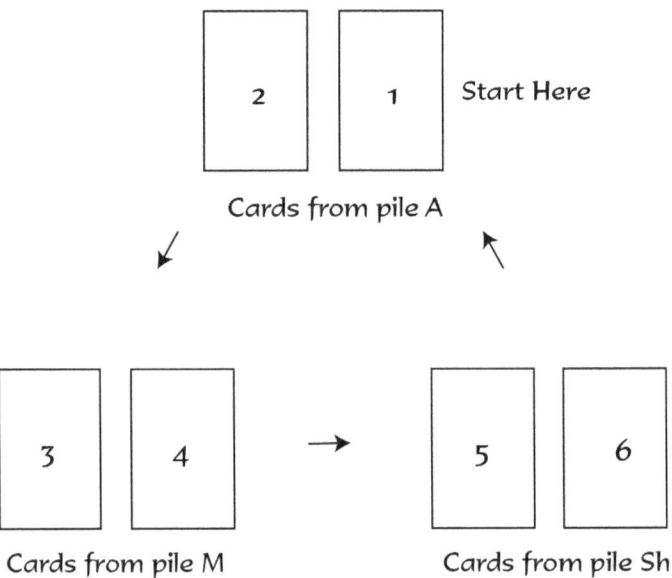

Three-card Layout.

1. Deal three cards — one at a time — face down into each place on the Triangle and discard the remainder.

2. Place the cards face up in the three-card layout as shown.

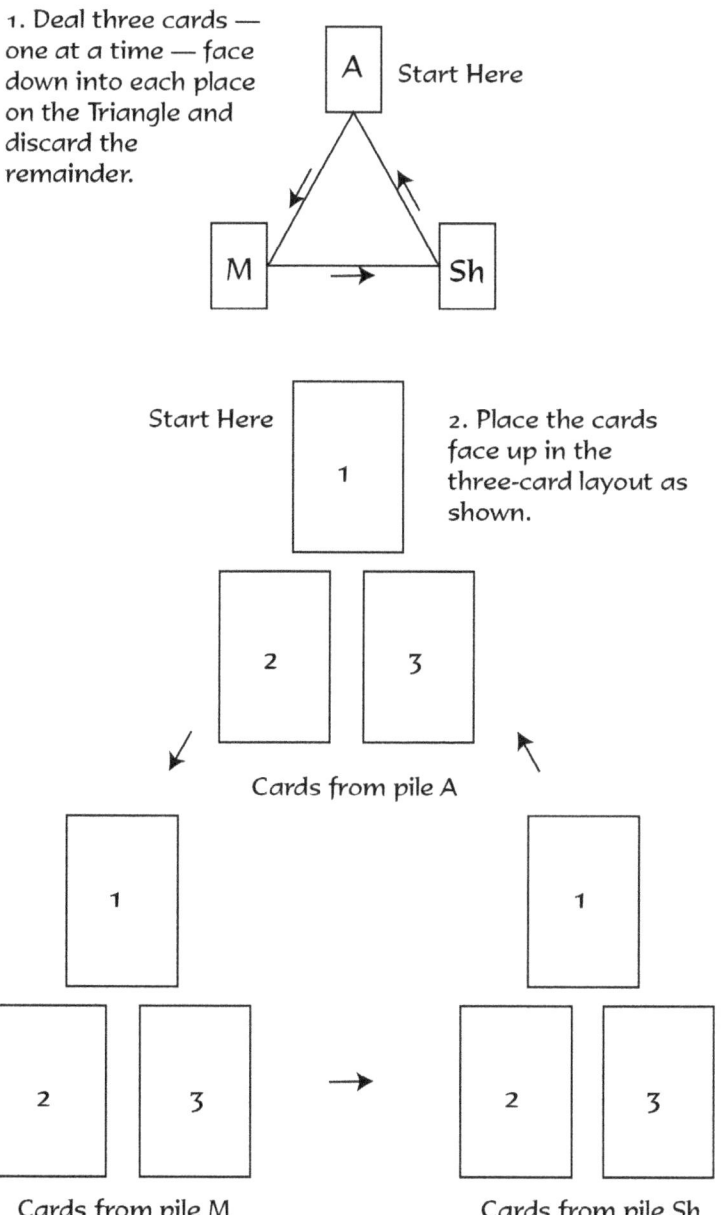

Cards from pile A

Cards from pile M

Cards from pile Sh

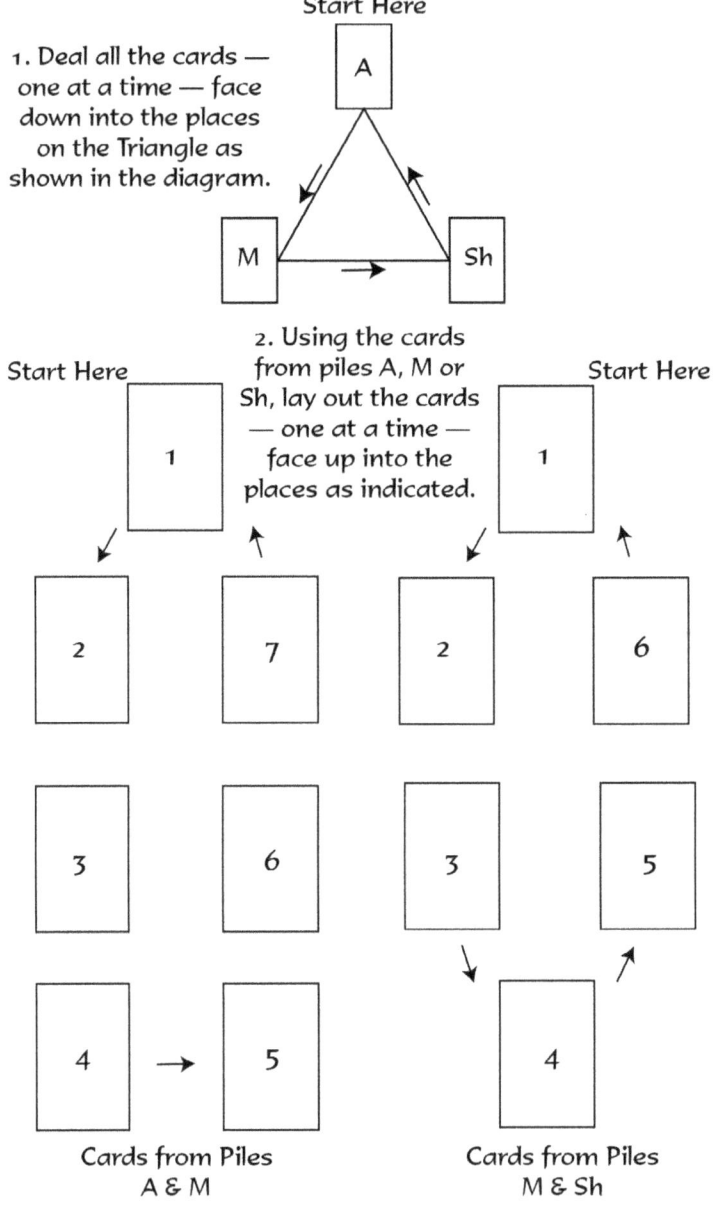

THE SECOND PROCEDURE

The Stone of the Wise

1. Do NOT formulate any question(s) when doing any of the preliminary procedures. This will require some effort on your part at first, especially if you have a favorite
[trusted] method already. But it is mandatory that you DO NOT formulate any question at this stage. Also, DO NOT choose a significator or a card to represent yourself. Of most importance — DO NOT consider any of the meanings of the cards! Simply lay out the cards as instructed and write down the cards that are in the layout.

Step One: Be still for 4 minutes and to the best of your ability, clear you mind of stressful and distracting thoughts. This is not meditation. The aim is to practice being still and calm for a few minutes.

Step Two: Shuffle the cards 7 times and deal the cards into the 4 piles as shown in the illustration. For the first 7 days use only the cards in pile# 1 in the Square. The next 7 days use only the cards from pile# 2 in the Square. The following 7 days use only the cards from pile#3 in the Square. The last 7 days use only the cards in pile#4 in the Square. Thus completing a 28 day cycle. Take note that piles 1&2 will have 20 cards while piles 3&4 will have 19.

Step Three: Using the chosen pile, shuffle the cards 9 times. Deal the cards into the Square as indicated in the illustration. For the first 7 days use only

the cards in the bottom right corner of the Square and layout the cards as indicated in the illustration.
The next 7 days use only the cards in the top right corner of the Square and layout the cards as indicated in the illustration.

The following 7 days use only the cards in the top left corner of the Square and layout the cards as indicated in the illustration.
The last 7 days use only the cards in the bottom left corner of the Square and layout the cards as indicated in the illustration. Note that when piles 1&2 are used each corner in the Square will have 5 cards. When piles 3&4 are used the bottom right corner and both top corners will have 5 cards and the bottom left corner will have 4 cards.

SECOND PROCEDURE

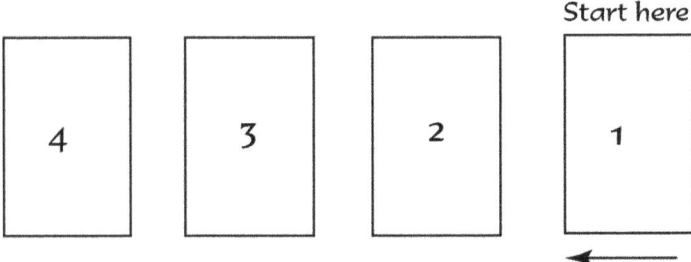

1. Shuffle the cards 7 times and deal the cards - one at a time - into the 4 piles as shown.

Note that when piles 1&2 are used each corner in the Square will have 5 cards. When piles 3&4 are used the bottom right corner and both top corners will have 5 cards and the bottom left corner will have 4 cards.

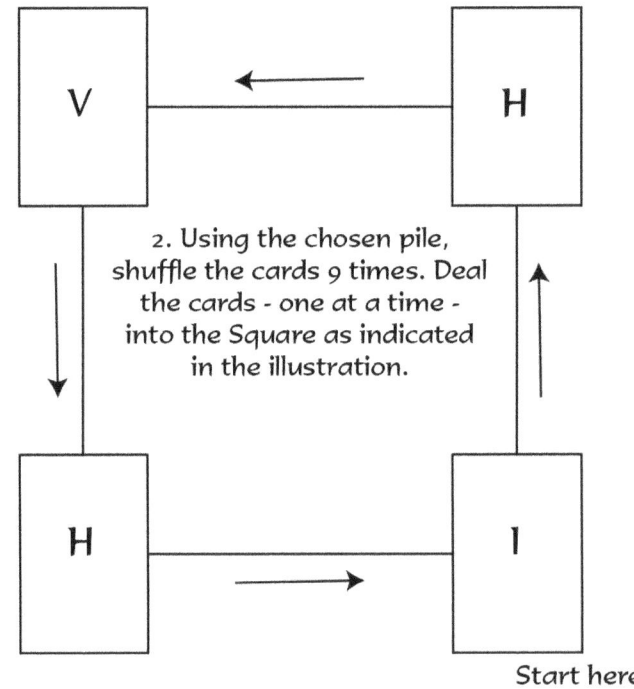

2. Using the chosen pile, shuffle the cards 9 times. Deal the cards - one at a time - into the Square as indicated in the illustration.

Second Procedure part 2
Layout for 5 cards

```
V ← H
↓     ↑
H  →  I
```

Using cards from piles I, H, V & H
Deal the cards face-up into the layout as indicated.

Start here

```
        1
       ↙ ↖
      2   5
      ↓   ↑
      3 → 4
```

Second Procedure part 2
Layout for 4 cards.

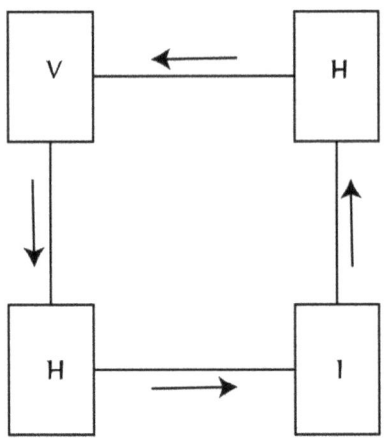

Using the cards from pile H.
Deal the cards face-up into the layout as indicated.

Start here

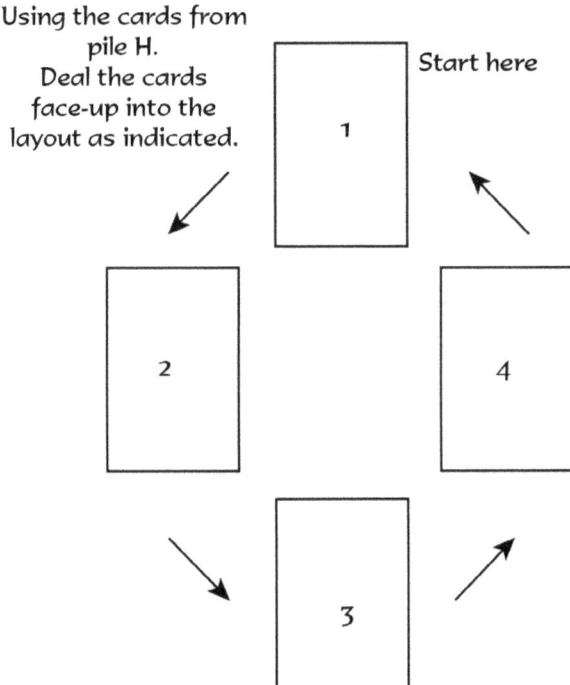

LIBERTARI / 13

THE THIRD PROCEDURE

The Circle of Perfection

1. Do NOT formulate any question(s) when doing any of the preliminary procedures. This will require some effort on your part at first, especially if you have a favorite
[trusted] method already. But it is mandatory that you DO NOT formulate any question at this stage. Also, DO NOT choose a significator or a card to represent yourself. Of most importance — DO NOT consider any of the meanings of the cards! Simply lay out the cards as instructed and write down the cards that are in the layout.

Step One: Be still for 7 minutes and to the best of your ability, clear your mind of stressful and distracting thoughts. This is not meditation. The aim is to practice being still and calm for a few minutes.

Step Two: Shuffle the cards 10 times and deal the cards into the 7 piles as shown in the illustration. For the first 7 days use only the cards in pile# 1 in the Circle. The next 7 days use only the cards from pile# 2 in the Circle. The following 7 days use only the cards from pile#3 in the Circle. The last 7 days use only the cards in pile#4 in the Circle. Thus completing a 28 day cycle. Take note that piles 1&2 will have 20 cards while piles 3&4 will have 19.

Step Three: Using the chosen pile, shuffle the cards
9 times. Deal the cards into the Circle as indicated in

the illustration. For the first 7 days layout the cards as indicated in the illustration. Place the first seven cards, one card at a time, [face up] into each pile in the circle. Discard the rest.

The next 7 days layout the cards as indicated in the illustration. Place the first seven cards, one card at a time,
[face up] into each pile in the circle. The next three cards are to be placed as shown in the illustration. The following 7 days layout the cards as indicated in the illustration. Place the first seven cards, one card at a time, [face up] into each pile in the circle. The next four cards are to be placed as shown in the illustration. The last 7 days layout the cards as indicated in the illustration. Repeat the layout used for the first seven days.

At the end of the three month preliminary training there needs to be a well kept record of ALL daily spread results. Keeping in mind the admonition "Man, Know Thyself!," the purpose of following All the steps in each procedure will now become apparent. It cannot be emphasized too strongly that the purpose of this instruction is not to assist the charlatans nor to entertain the idly curious.

THIRD PROCEDURE
First Part

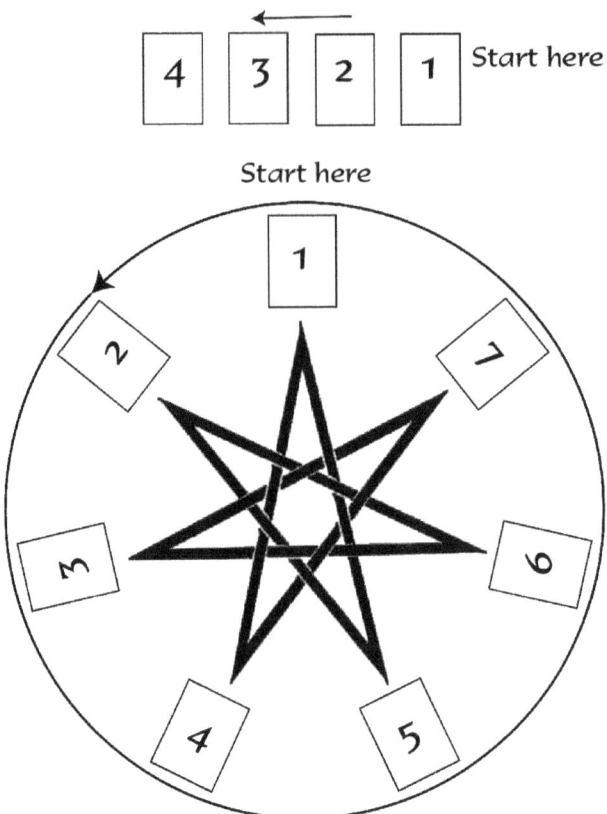

Deal the cards into the Circle as indicated in the illustration.

For the **first 7 days** lay out the cards as indicated in the illustration. Place the first seven cards, one card at a time, [face up] into each place in the circle. Discard the rest.

THIRD PROCEDURE
part two

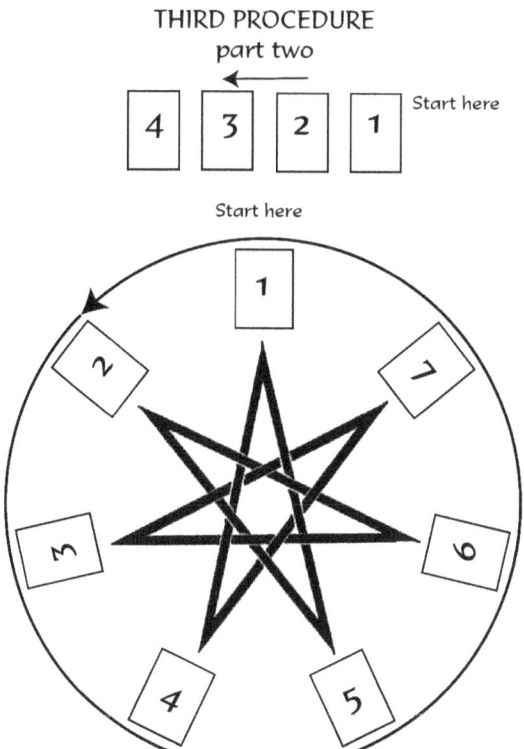

The **next 7 days** lay out the cards as indicated. Place the first seven cards, one card at a time, [face up] into each pile in the circle. The next three cards are to be placed as shown in the illustration.

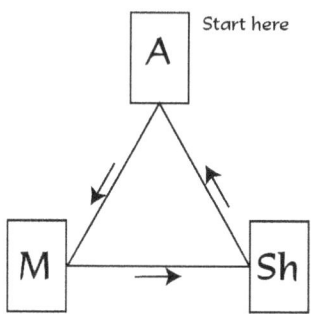

THIRD PROCEDURE
part three

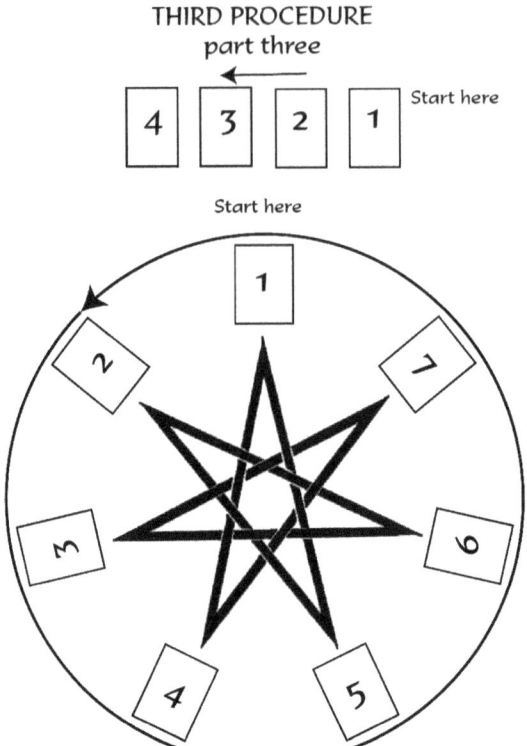

The **following 7 days** lay out the cards as indicated. Place the first seven cards, one card at a time, [face up] into each pile in the circle. The next four cards are to be placed as shown in the illustration. The **last 7 days repeat** the layout used for the **first seven days**.

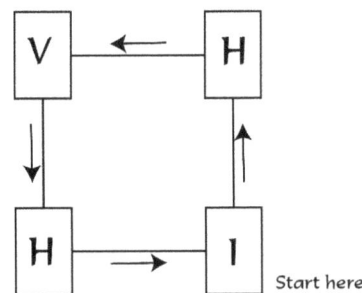

ENDURA / 12

ROSE LIGHT ORACLE METHOD

The preparatory stage of training now begins. Examine your three month record of spreads and look for any repeated patterns — frequency of occurrence — within each procedure and between the procedures. Make note of them in your records. As you examine your records think of any experiences in your life that were not of the ordinary / mundane kind and on what days they occurred. Re-examine the spread(s) for those days. Decide which procedure has yielded the closest indicator of those experiences being a possibility. By viewing the records in this way, in retrospect
— there is less of a tendency to project meanings onto the reading. Be sure to keep an active and accurate record of all of this.

Now — for your daily practice — combine the first and second procedures — The Trigonem Igneum and Stone of the Wise. Again, No question is to be formulated and No significator is to be used. Use the layout format as shown. Record your results. Continue with this practice for one full month.

At the end of this period examine your records and repeat the analysis procedure given. The next month the Circle of Perfection is to be added to the practice for one month. Continue with the examination and analysis of your records as described at the month's end.

Daily Practice part 1 [first month]

For the first 7 days use the cards from pile #1, the next 7 days use the cards from pile #2, the following 7 days use the cards from pile #3 and the last 7 days use the cards from pile #4.
Always begin by being still for 3 minutes.
Shuffle the cards 7 times.
Step one: Deal the cards — one at a time into the four piles as indicated.
Step two: Using the chosen pile deal the first seven cards — one at a time face up into the layout as shown.
Step three: Record the results.

Daily Practice part 2 [second month]

For the first 7 days use the cards from pile #1, the next 7 days use the cards from pile #2, the following 7 days use the cards from pile #3 and the last 7 days use the cards from pile #4.
Always begin by being still for 3 minutes. Shuffle the cards 7 times.
Step one: Deal the cards — one at a time into the four piles as indicated.
Step two: Using the chosen pile deal the first fourteen cards — one at a time — face up into the layout as shown.
Step three: Record the results.

Step one: Deal the cards — one at a time into the four piles as indicated.

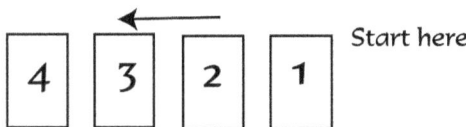

Step two: Using the chosen pile deal the first seven cards — one at a time, face up into the layout as shown. First three into Triangle and the next four into Square.

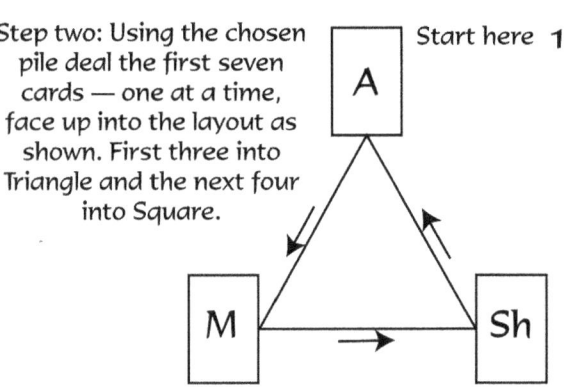

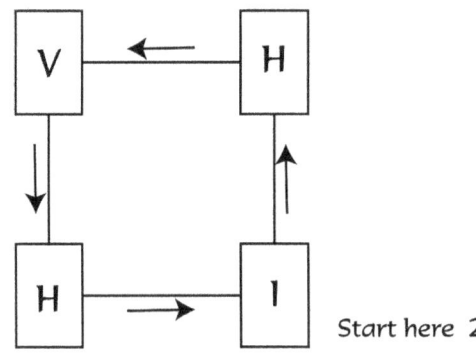

Step one: Deal the cards — one at a time into the four piles as indicated.

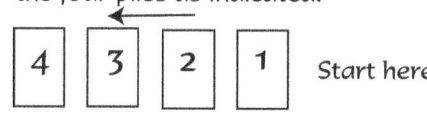

Start here

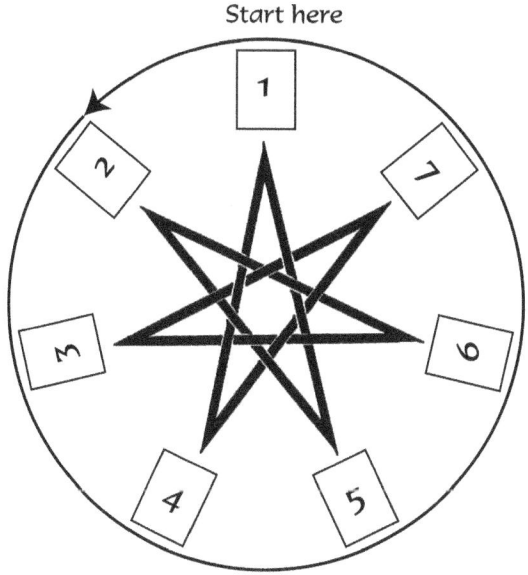

Step two: Using the chosen pile deal the first fourteen cards — one at a time — face up into the layout as shown:
1. Circle 2. Triangle 3. Square

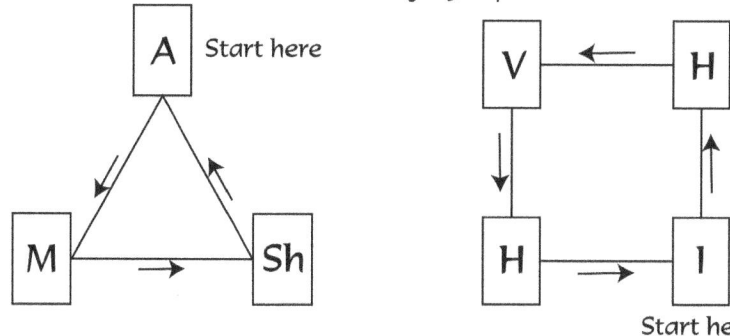

Start here

Preparation for utilizing the Rose-Light Oracle method requires that the 5 month training be followed faithfully. At the end of the 5 months one can decide which 'petal' — Trigonem Igneum, Stone of the Wise, Circle of Perfection — to use and when. A complete divine is the full Circle of Perfection procedure.

DIVINATORY IMPLICATIONS OF THE MAJOR ARCANA

The following is a brief summary of divinatory implications of the Tarot cards. Some of this information is gathered from the writings of Paul F. Case both published and unpublished.

Traditionally, the Tarot is divided into two sections known as the Major and Minor Arcana. The Major Arcana consists of 22 cards and forms a distinct group by itself. Some decks correlate the 22 Major Arcana cards to the 22 Hebrew letters. Some decks have the Major Arcana marked, each with a Hebrew letter. There has been a difference of opinion among certain authorities as to the numbering of the Major Arcana cards, this discussion has centered around the numbering of the Fool, whether to assign the zero sign or the number one as well as where to place it in the deck; at the beginning or after the World. For the purpose of this instruction, the Fool card receives the number 0 and the World card the number 21. With the Fool being assigned zero, it can be seen that it can be placed anywhere in the deck and not run the risk of being out of sequence.

The Rose Light deck is of recent design and it is designed specifically for use with the Rose-Light Oracle method. The images comprising the Rose-Light deck have come about as a result of inner instruction. However it is not necessary to have this deck in order to make use of the method. All true students of Tarot may make use of the Rose-Light method. The instruction given in this lesson holds true for the traditional Tarot cards as well. It should be noted that use of the word 'traditional' indicates such Tarot images as found on the Rider-Waite Tarot or the Tarot of Paul Foster Case. The titles of the cards in the Rose-Light deck are different than the Traditional in most cases. A brief list of attributes for the 22 Major Arcana will be given.

THE MAJOR ARCANA

In the Rose-Light deck the symbolism follows the tradition of the Tarot in the sense of the use that is made of the images. In our consideration of the Major Arcana we will divide it into three sections; this division is based on the qualities of the 22 Hebrew letters which were assigned thereto.

In Qabalistic cosmology the 22 letters are the building blocks of creation. There are 3 Mother letters which are considered as the first elements or fundamentals. There are 7 Double letters which depict the antithesis to which human life is exposed and there are 12 Simple letters which constitute the boundaries of the created universe.

The three Mother letters contain the fundamental Law of Equilibrium. The three Mothers are: Aleph (A), Ox, (see chart on correlation of letters to cards), Mem (M), Water, and Shin (Sh), Fang. Mem(M) and Shin(Sh) are a pair of scales and Aleph(A) is always the point of equilibrium between them. They represent the ideas of active and passive with one equilibrative force between them. The key to reconciling all pairs of opposites is contained in the knowledge of the three Mother letters; active and passive, fixed and volatile, positive and negative — all are represented by either Mem(M) or Shin(Sh) with Aleph(A) as the one mediating or reconciling influence between them.

The seven double letters (see chart): Beth[B], House — Gimel[G] Camel — Daleth[D], Door — Kaph[K], Hand (closed) — Peh[P], Mouth — Resh[R], Face and Tau[T, Th], Cross — depict the thesis and antithesis of Life and Death, Peace and Strife, Wisdom and Folly, Wealth and Poverty, Grace and Sin, Fertility and Sterility, Dominion and Slavery. The seven doubles represent three pairs of opposites with one reconciler holding them in balance. There is the Height and Depth, East and West, North and South and the Palace of Holiness at the center which is their foundation.

The twelve simple letters represent the functions of consciousness manifesting in humanity as: seeing, hearing, smelling, speaking, tasting, coition, working, locomotion, anger, mirth, meditation, and sleeping. They are six pairs of opposites continually seeking equilibrium. They are of equal strength and arranged around a circle. They are twelve in number and their circle makes a complete unity or 13.

There are the twelve constellations and the Sun which visits them all. The twelve simples depict the twelve oblique points which establish the boundaries of the world. The twelve simples are the twelve constellations in the world. They are the twelve months in the year. In Man they are the twelve personality types male and female.

CONCERNING THE PILES NUMBERED 1-2-3-4

The first pile involves the ideas connected with the Yod of Yod Heh Vau Heh, and the attributions related to the world of Atziluth along with all the correspondences related to it. In essence it is about the beginning of some enterprise or business to be undertaken; The main or root-idea behind some matter. The question is directed more toward causes than with outward conditions. Depending on the individual, the cards in this pile, might involve matters of a higher spiritual life. When using the cards from this pile, all Wands in the layout have special emphasis.

Cards in the second pile should have a general significance involving ideas connected with the first Heh of Yod Heh Vau Heh and the attributions related to the world of Briah along with all the correspondences related to it. In essence, the question will involve desires and wishes in the formulation of plans; Possibly the question will concern the state of the emotions or affections or a matter in which higher feelings are deeply affected, such as a love affair. When using the cards from this pile, all Cups in the layout have special emphasis.

If using cards from the third pile, the question is related to ideas linked with the Vau of Yod Heh Vau Heh, and the attributions related to the world of Yetzirah as well as all the correspondences related to it. In essence, the question will be about what one should do or what action should be taken to bring about a particular result, to evade or overcome some conflict

with others; a lawsuit or similar encounter.
The question will be somehow connected with disharmony, either actual or threatened; possibly it will involve the health. When using the cards from this pile, all Swords have special importance.

With cards found in the fourth pile, the question involves the ideas connected with the second Heh in Yod Heh Vau Heh, and the attributions related to the world of Assiah along with all the correspondences related to it. In essence, the question will involve things of the outer world; practical life; in general, all material affairs such as financial matters, money, property, business, real estate, et cetera. When using the cards from this pile, all Coins have particular value.

CONCERNING TRIGONEM IGNEUM

Generally speaking, it is usual that information is sought concerning a human life, or perhaps an event; a person or occasion or occurrence. In consideration of these circumstances, Time is of principle significance. In Tarot divination time is divided into three great periods: 1. Past, [Sh]; 2. Present, [A]; 3. Future, [M].
With cards found in pile number one — Sh, the basis of the problem is related to past activities, thoughts, feelings. If found in pile number two — A, one is dealing with a condition that is presently occurring; Resolution of the situation requires attending to the matter here and now. For the third pile — M, the main circumstances of the problem will be encountered in the future, as will results.

Concerning Stone of the Wise In addition to the divisions of Past, Present and Future, there are also in a Life or an Event four great periods of progress or evolution: In a Life: 1. Childhood — 2. Youth — 3. Maturity — 4. Old Age. In an Event: 1. Beginning — 2. Climax — 3. Decline, Obstacles — 4. Fall, End.

According to which pile is used, the implication of the reading will be indicative of what stage of development the situation under consideration has reached.

CONCERNING CIRCLE OF PERFECTION

The two procedures — Trigonem Igneum and Stone of the Wise are to be mastered before attempting a complete divine — Circle of Perfection. The third operation combines the essence of the first two and adds a third procedure.

It is important to remember that at all times during the divination, what is under consideration is in truth, the activity of Spirit. This Spirit is the true life of all things in manifestation. What divination attempts is to get a "glimpse" of Spirit in operation in a particular field of expression. The circle has been used as a symbol for Spirit by all the schools of the Mysteries.

The complete divine — Circle of Perfection, depicts the operation of Spirit through the "Seven Churches" which are in Assiah. This divination is performed independently of the first two procedures however, it may also be used in conjunction with them. Assess the nature of the reading according to the location of the cards. Where the card is placed indicates which of the seven centers is involved. Location 1: Ephesus — Dominion / Slavery / Saturn

Location 2: Pergamos — Wealth / Poverty / Jupiter
Location 3: Sardis — Wisdom / Folly / Venus
Location 4: Laodiceans — Life / Death / Mercury
Location 5: Smyrna — Grace / Sin / Mars
Location 6: Thyatira — Fertility / Sterility / Sun
Location 7: Philadelphia — Peace / Strife / Moon

The four piles refer to the four great periods of progress or evolution --- in Life and in the World.

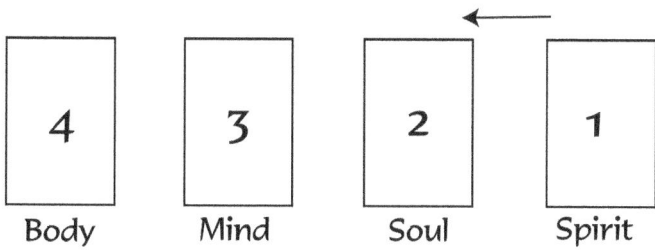

In Tarot divination time is divided into three great periods: 1. Past, [Sh]; 2. Present, [A]; 3. Future, [M].

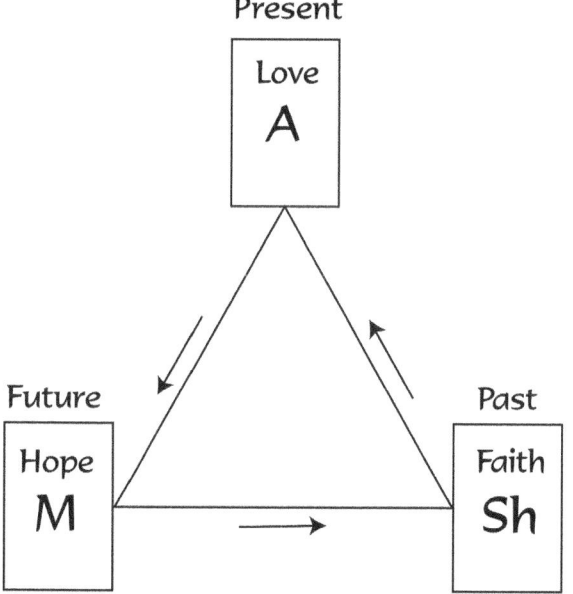

With cards found in pile — Sh, the basis of the problem is related to past activities, thoughts, feelings. If found in pile — A, one is dealing with a condition that is presently occurring; Resolution of the situation requires attending to the matter here and now. For the pile — M, the main circumstances of the problem will be encountered in the future, as will results.

FIRST PROCEDURE
Two-card Layout / Affinity of cards
according to location

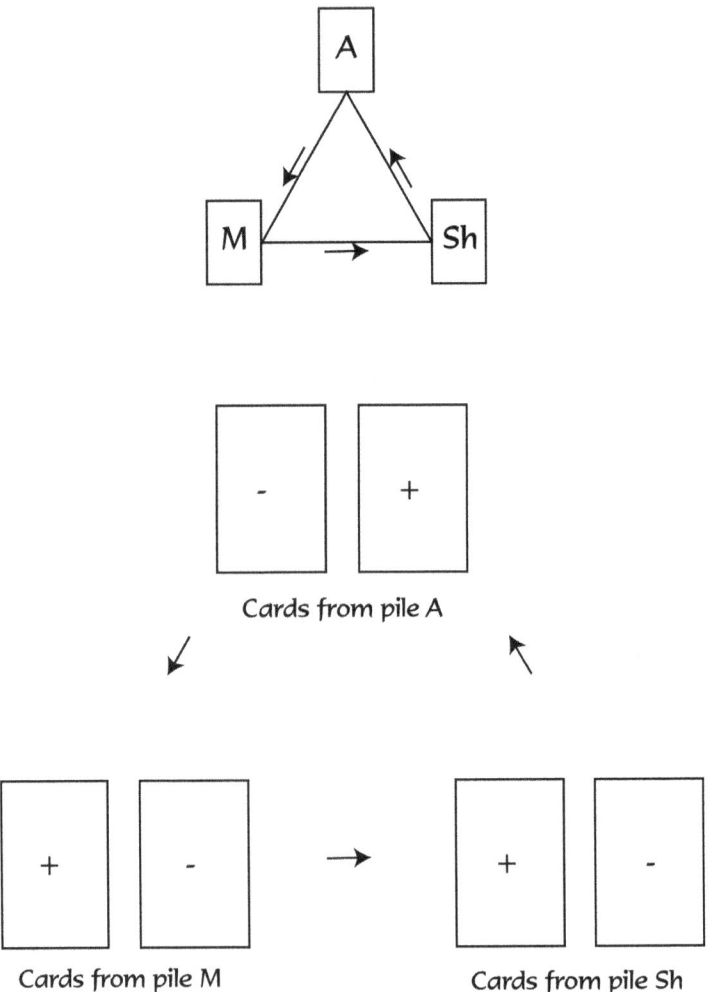

FIRST PROCEDURE
Three-card Layout / Affinity of cards according to location

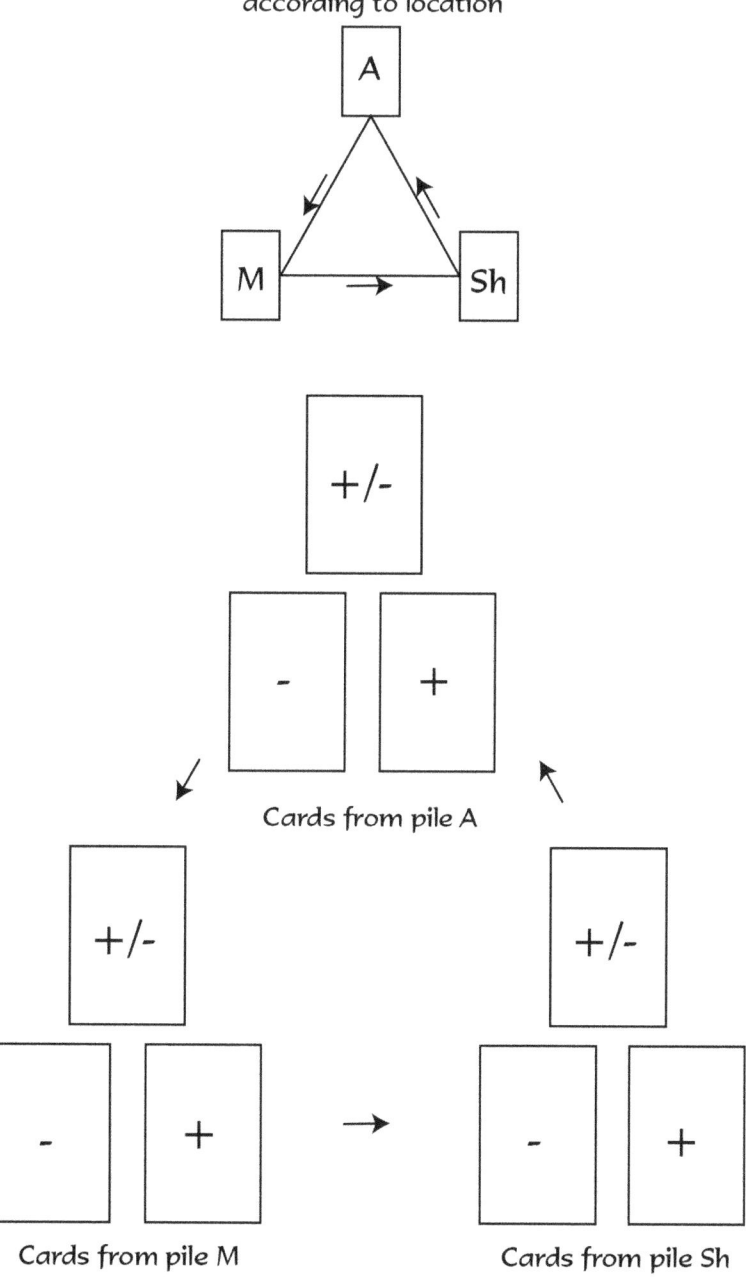

FIRST PROCEDURE
Full Layout.

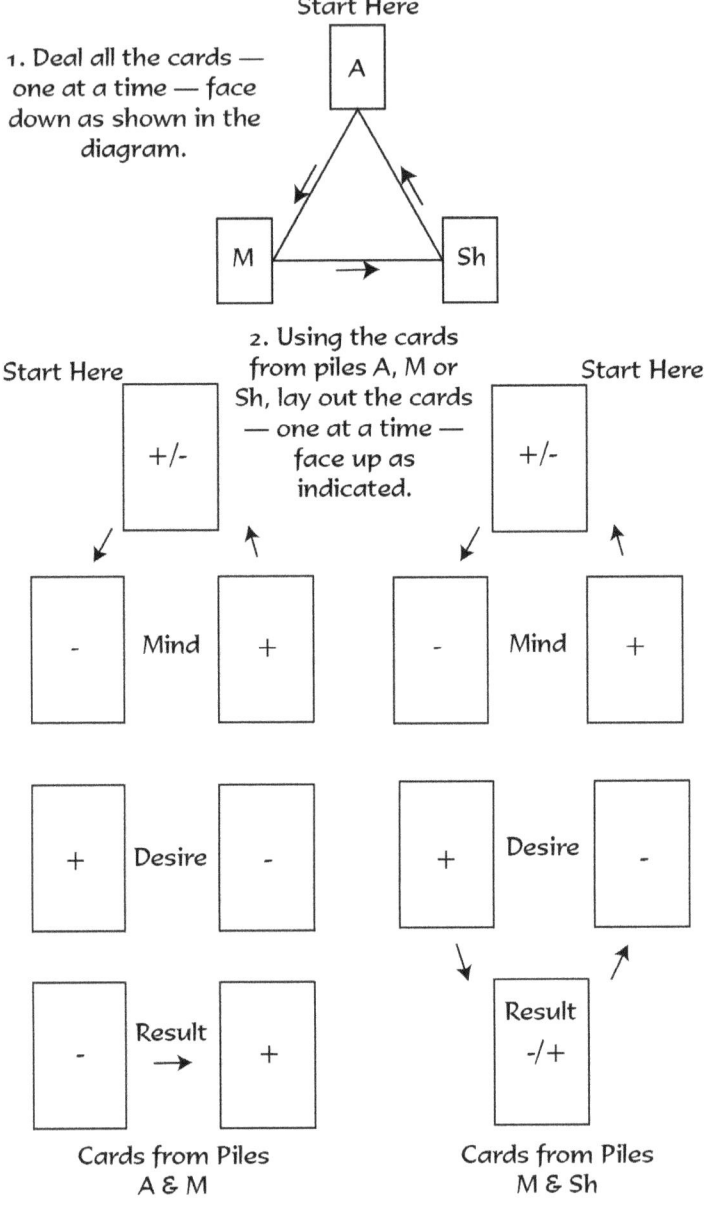

SECOND PROCEDURE

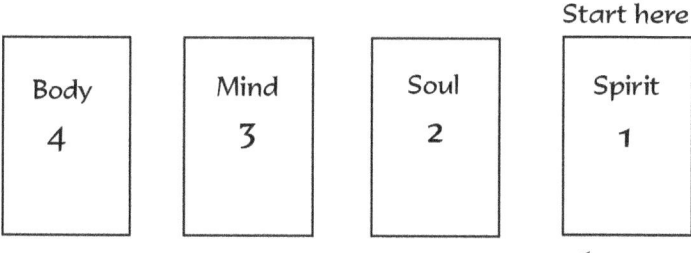

1. Shuffle the cards 7 times and deal the cards - one at a time - into the 4 piles as shown.

Note that when piles 1&2 are used each corner in the Square will have 5 cards. When piles 3&4 are used the bottom right corner and both top corners will have 5 cards and the bottom left corner will have 4 cards.

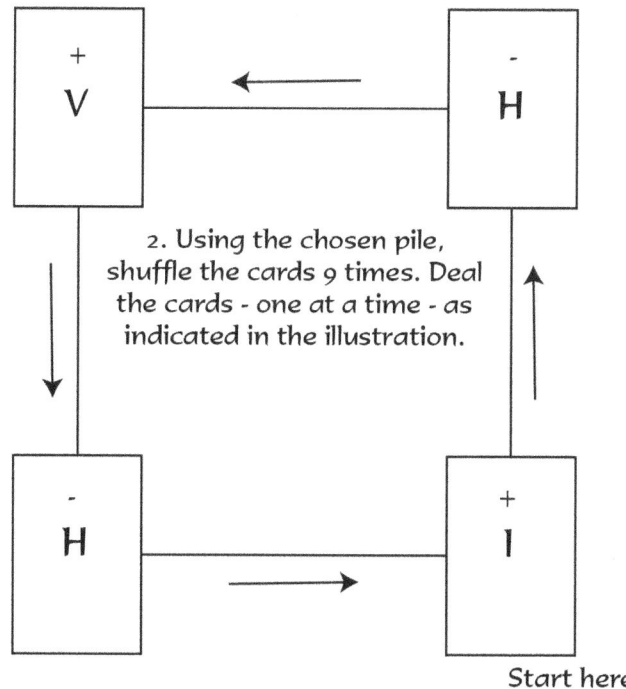

2. Using the chosen pile, shuffle the cards 9 times. Deal the cards - one at a time - as indicated in the illustration.

The four piles refer to the four great periods of progress or evolution --- in Life and in the World.

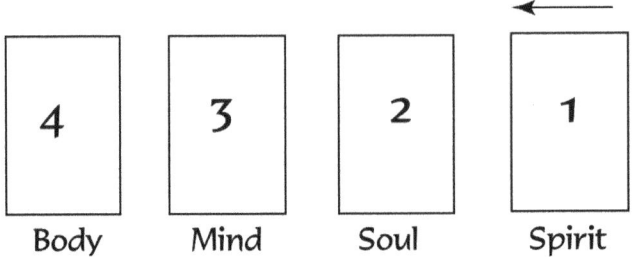

The four great periods of progress or evolution: In a Life, 1. Childhood; 2. Youth; 3. Maturity; 4. Old Age.
In an Event, 1. Beginning; 2. Climax; 3. Decline, Obstacles; 4. Fall, End.

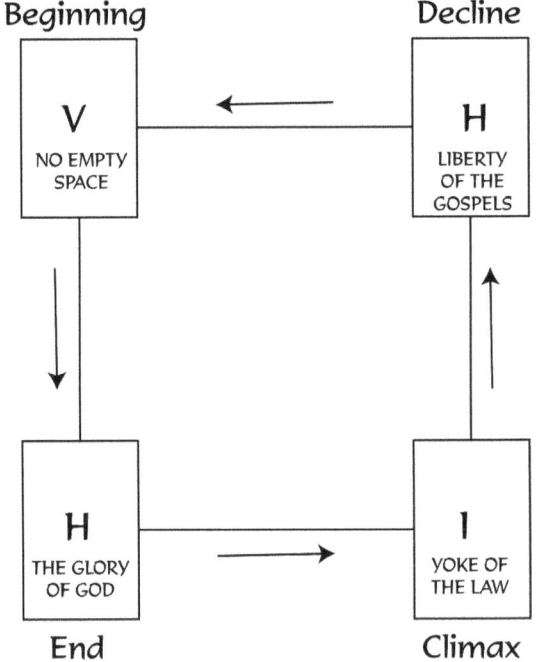

Second Procedure part 2
Layout for 5 cards

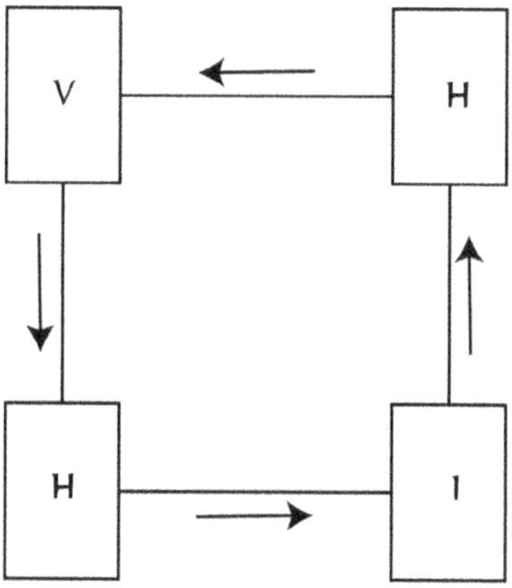

```
    V  ←————  H
    │          ↑
    ↓          │
    H  ————→  I
```

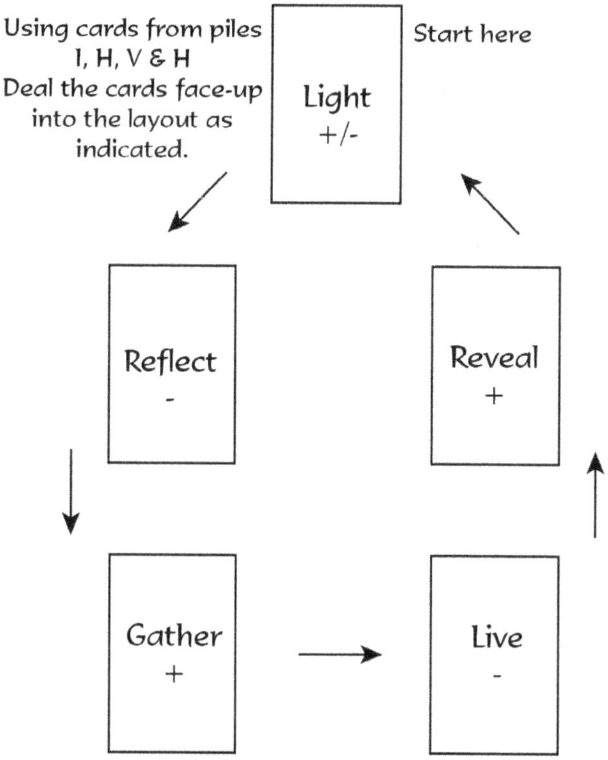

Using cards from piles
I, H, V & H
Deal the cards face-up
into the layout as
indicated.

Start here

Light
+/-

Reflect
-

Reveal
+

Gather
+

Live
-

143

Second Procedure part 2
Layout for 4 cards.

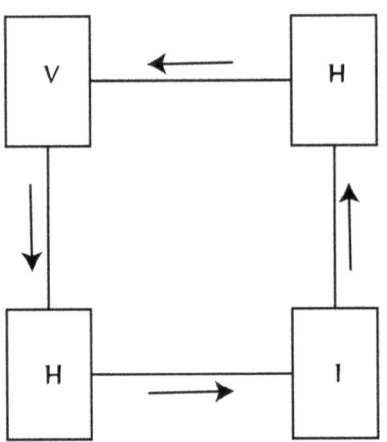

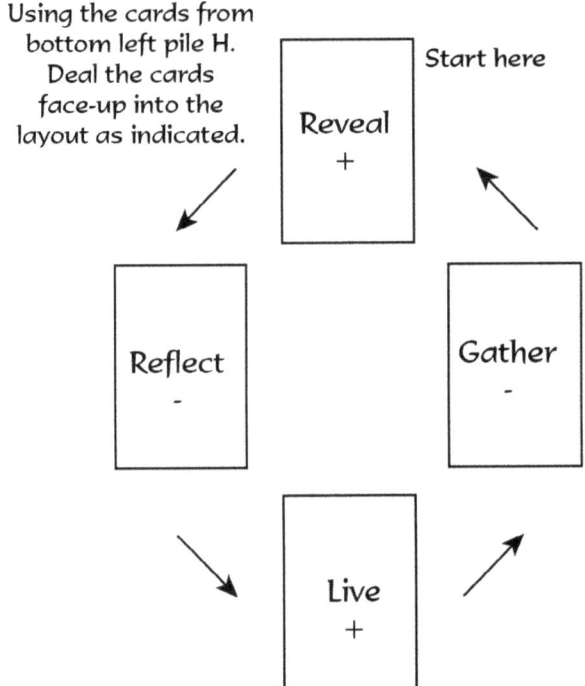

Using the cards from bottom left pile H. Deal the cards face-up into the layout as indicated.

The complete divine — Circle of Perfection, depicts the operation of Spirit through the "Seven Churches" which are in Assiah.

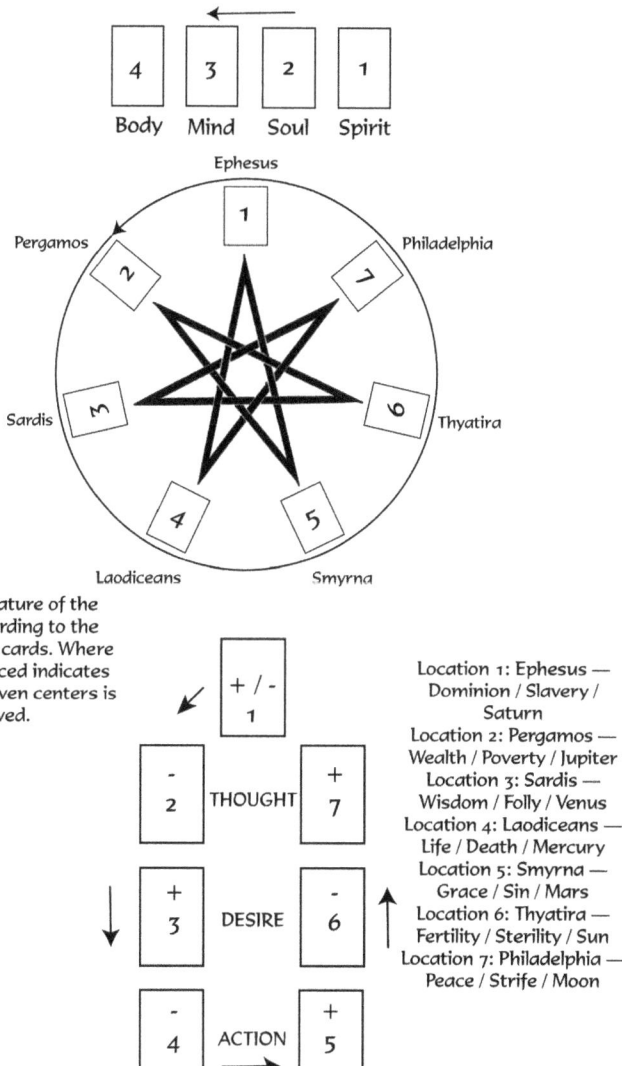

Assess the nature of the reading according to the location of the cards. Where the card is placed indicates which of the seven centers is involved.

Location 1: Ephesus — Dominion / Slavery / Saturn
Location 2: Pergamos — Wealth / Poverty / Jupiter
Location 3: Sardis — Wisdom / Folly / Venus
Location 4: Laodiceans — Life / Death / Mercury
Location 5: Smyrna — Grace / Sin / Mars
Location 6: Thyatira — Fertility / Sterility / Sun
Location 7: Philadelphia — Peace / Strife / Moon

ROSE-LIGHT ORACLE METHOD
Complete Divine
Circle of Perfection

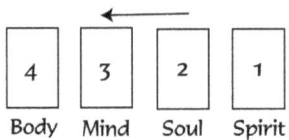

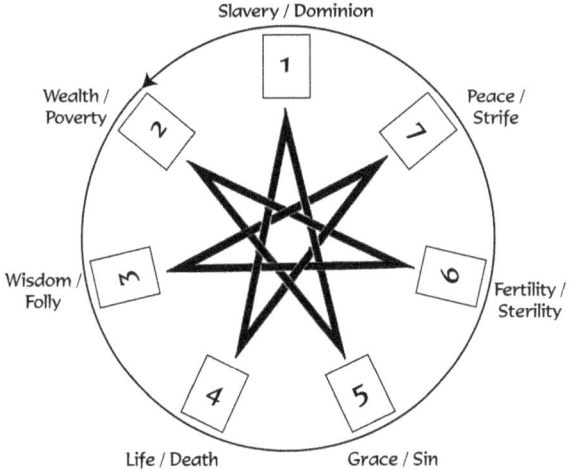

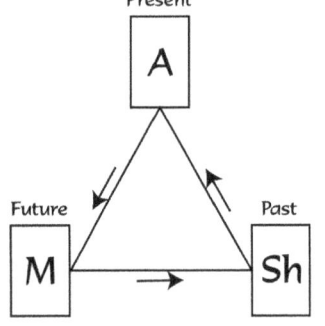
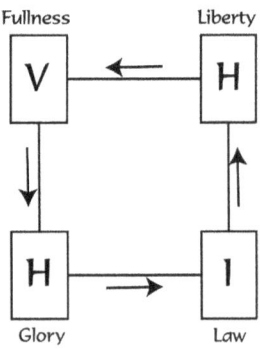

ROSE-LIGHT ORACLE METHOD
Complete Divine
Circle of Perfection

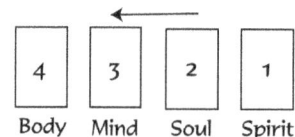

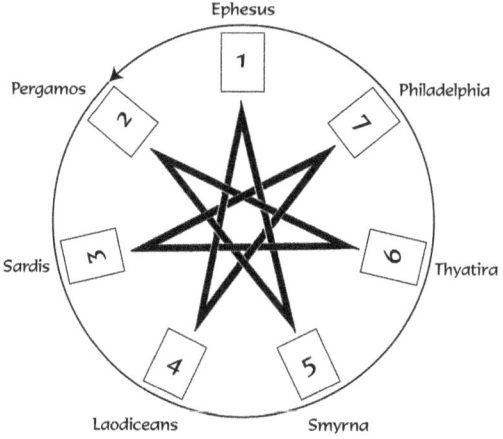

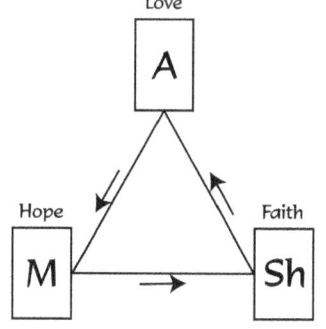

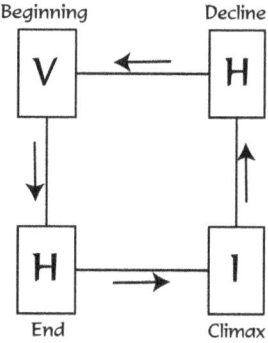

CHART OF AFFINITY

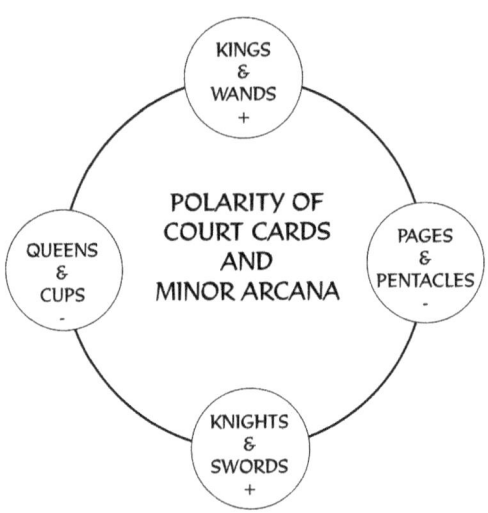

POLARITY OF MAJOR ARCANA

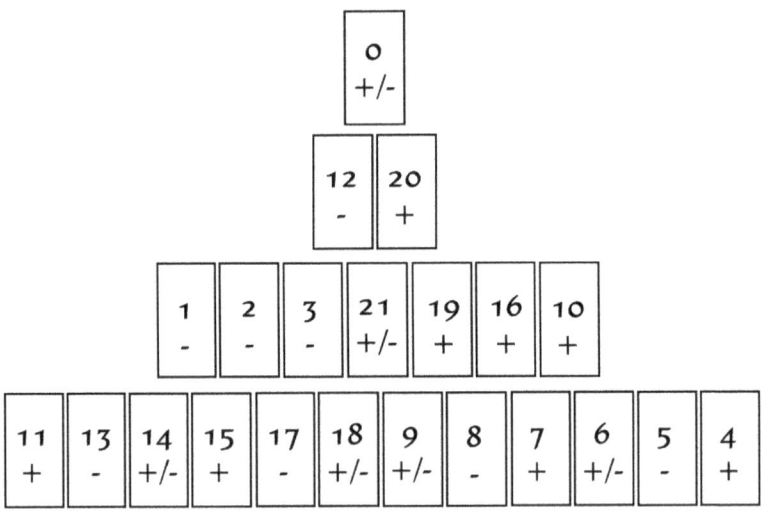

Oracle Method

The first seven cards form the Circle of Perfection, the next three form the Trigonem Igneum and the last four cards make the Stone of the Wise.

Wherever the cards are placed their weight is judged by their affinity with the location (see chart). Cards placed in the circle, indicate which one of the seven centers is involved. The locations in the circle indicate a state of transition — seeking eqilibrium. The matter under consideration involves some necessary change in the Querent's life.

Position one on the wheel: limitation, restriction; the necessity to confront problems and overcome resistance.
Position two on the wheel: lack, insecurity; the necessity to establish order in one's life.
Position three on the wheel: loss, defeat; the necessity to overcome daydreaming and idle wishes.
Position four on the wheel: ignorance, prejudice; the necessity to develop the ability live in the present.
Position five on the wheel: destruction, death; the necessity to control temper and the tendency to take offense.
Position six on the wheel: illness, depression; the necessity to learn to serve.
Position seven on the wheel: guilt, remorse; the necessity to learn to forgive.

Cards placed in the triangle concern the operations of consciousness regarding some action or event.

Position A in the triangle: The operation of higher intelligence. Effort will result in being attuned to a higher level of awareness and more Light to bear.
Position Sh in the triangle: The operation of self-consciousness. An error in thinking. Correct reasoning required in regards to the situation.
Position M in the triangle: The operation of sub-consciousness. Ignorance and delusion rooted in some habit pattern, some manner of response that is automatic.

Cards placed in square depict the type and level of energy affecting the Querent.

Position I in the square: Influenced by the energy of the highest plane, the realm of spirit. In this location, life is under the direction of the Spiritual Hierarchy and whatever problem is manifesting, is a result of the Hierarchy bringing certain forces to bear on the Querent.
Position H (top right) in the square: The energy involved is from the level of the creative plane. In this location, the problem lies with the emotions and feelings; in essence, whatever desires are troubling the Querent, they are an indication of the imbalance in the energy field of this plane. Generally, this location indicates depression and uncontrolled mood changes.
Position V in the square: The energy of the astral plane is represented. In this location, the Querent is under the influence of the astral world and the various entities abiding therein. The basis of the problem

involves the inability to establish any definite sense of purpose. Generally, this location indicates inconsistent, changing, somewhat "flighty" thought processes.

Position H (lower left) in the square: The energy of the material plane. This location indicates that the Querent is mesmerized by the illusions of the physical world. The essence of the problem is that he/she is attached to materialistic values and finds no comfort in "things unseen." Generally, this location indicates gross and carnal appetites; greed, avarice, and laziness are also indicated.

SYMBOLISM

The numbered cards as well as the court-cards of each suit represent the activities of the world to which they correspond. Some traditional number symbolism is necessary to make use of the Minor Arcana. The following is by no means a complete listing of the various esoteric meanings of numbers, but it is sufficient for the purposes of this instruction. Number symbols represent truths immanent in all things and manifest in all phenomena. The science of number is the foundation of every other department of human knowledge. Study well the information concerning number in this instruction. The information given is essential in the preparation of your mind to understand the principles and laws which you will apply to begin bringing yourself into harmony with the rhythms of Cosmos.

Do not be discouraged by some imagined inaptitude or dislike for mathematics. It does not require that you be a "math whiz" or have a "natural ability" with figures and abstract reasoning. It takes little time to master the main points of the symbolism. Practice will aid you in becoming proficient in the various applications of the principles.

The numeral symbols from 0 to 9, represent successive stages in every cycle of the Life-power's self-expression, from the grand scale of Cosmos to the smaller scale of personal unfoldment. The order in the numeral series reflects an order which prevails throughout creation.

Thus Tradition tells us that the Supreme Architect of the Universe has ordered all things by number, measure and weight. The properties of number are evident everywhere, from the whirling of electrons within the atom, to the arrangement of parts in a living body.

Some of the attributions may not seem clear at first. Some may even appear arbitrary or require a "stretch of the imagination." Do not give up. Keep your purpose in view. You are learning number symbols because they are the basis of the Magical Language used by initiates to transmit their knowledge from generation to generation.

Even if the symbols were arbitrary (which they are not), you must know their traditional interpretations in order to understand the Esoteric Language of the Mysteries. No satisfactory substitute for this language has been devised. By means of it, two initiates may have a long conversation even though neither knows a word of the other's native language. They would be able to express more meaning by means of a few lines and figures than could be put into pages of words.

0 - NO-THING: The limitless, undefined Power which is before all creation; the unknown - immeasurable - infinite - eternal Source; the Rootless Root of all manifestation; ab-sence of quantity, quality, or mass; The Limitless Light; The Ellipse of Eternity; The Cosmic Egg; Supra-consciousness.

1 - BEGINNING: This number is considered first in the series of digits since zero symbolizes that which precedes all manifestation and thus is not included in any series; inception - initiative - the Primal Will - selection - unity - singleness -individuality - attention - one-pointedness - concentration -the definite or manifest, as contrasted with the indefinable Source; Self-awareness. Kether, the Crown. Spiritual plane; Divine Self.

2 - DUPLICATION: Repetition; Wisdom and Science; opposition - polarity - antithesis - succession - sequence - continuation - diffusion - separation - radiation -secondariness - subordination - dependence - Sub-consciousness. Chokmah, Wisdom. Causal plane; Divine Life.

3 - MULTIPLICATION: Increase - growth - augmentation - expansion - amplification - extension - productiveness -fecundity - generation - the response of subconscious mental activity to self-conscious impulse in the generation of mental images - hence, Understanding. Binah, Understanding. Causal plane; Divine Mind.

4 - ORDER: System - regulation - management - supervision - control - authority; command - dominance - the classifying activity of self-consciousness (this is induced by conscious response to sub-conscious mental imagery) - the Cosmic Order, Reason. Chesed,

Mercy. Higher mental plane; Memory.

    5 - MEDIATION: Mediation is an idea suggested by the fact that five is the middle term in the series of signs from 1 to 9. Adaptation - intervention - adjustment - hence, Justice; accommodation - reconciliation - result of the classifying activities symbolized by subconscious elaboration of these classifications and the formation of deductions therefrom. Projected into the field of self-conscious awareness, these deductions are what are termed intuitions. Geburah, Justice. Higher mental plane; Volition.

    6 - RECIPROCATION: Interchange - correlation - response - coordination - cooperation - correspondence - harmony - concord - equilibration - symmetry - Beauty. Tiphareth, Beauty. Egoic plane; Central Self.

    7 - EQUILIBRIUM: Is the result of equilibration. The concrete application of the laws of symmetry and reciprocation. Mastery - poise - rest - conquest - peace - safety - art - security - Victory. Netzach, Victory. Lower mental plane; Desire.

    8 - RHYTHM: Periodicity - alternation - vibration - pulsation - flux and reflux - involution and evolution -education - culture - the response of subconsciousness to everything symbolized by seven. Hod, Splendor. Lower mental plane; Intellect.

    9 - CONCLUSION: The literal meaning is "closing together." This implies the union of elements that are separate until the conclusion is reached. Goal; end - completion - fulfillment, attainment - the final result of the process symbolized by the series of digits - perfection - adeptship,"Three times Three." Yesod, Foundation. Astral plane; Vital soul.

When dealing with numbers of two or more digits, consider the combined meanings of each of the number symbols. Always begin with the digit on the right. In the number ten, zero may be thought of as the power expressing through the agency of one. Ten comes after nine and this implies that nine stands for a finality which refers to a single cycle of evolution only.

The completion of a cycle is always a return to the Eternal No-Thing — zero, but since zero is essentially changeless in its inherent nature, the Eternal Source is eternally a self-manifesting power. Consequently, a new cycle begins as soon as the preceding cycle ends.

10 - EMBODIMENT: The Kingdom - Law in action - the ever-turning wheel of manifestation - the eternal creativeness of the Life-power - the incessant whirling forth of the Self-expression of the Primal Will. Malkuth, Kingdom. Physical plane; Body.

The exact meaning of any Minor Card may therefore be determined from its suit, combined with its name (if a court-card), or its number.

Esoteric Implications Of The Hebrew Letters

THE THREE MOTHERS

Aleph [A] is the first Mother and means ox. Being the first Mother, Aleph symbolizes the intangible air from which the One I Am brought forth the existence out of nothing.

Aleph connects the first Sephirah Kether — the Crown, with the second Sephirah Chokmah — Wisdom. The Intelligence assigned to Aleph is Scintillating or Fiery and carries the ideas of brightness, clearness, splendor. In Alchemy, Aleph represents the primal element Air. Esoteric Astrology assigns the planet Uranus to the Aleph. The numerical value of Aleph is 1. The Aleph symbolizes the influence of the Primal Intent at the beginning of a cycle of manifestation.

Mem [M] is the second Mother and means water. Mem connects the sephirah Geburah —Severity, with the sephirah Hod — Splendor. Mem is the path through which the Volition of the Higher Self influences the intellectual functions of the personality and is what gives the individual the sense of
self-will. Mem is the 23rd path of Wisdom and is called the Stable Intelligence; and it carries the ideas of "duration" or "existence." Esoteric Astrology assigns the planet Neptune to Mem. This card also represents the alchemical "First Matter" which is the primal Water. The numerical value of Mem is 40.

Shin [Sh] is the third Mother and means tooth or fang. Shin connects the sephirah Hod — Splendor, with the sephirah Malkuth — Kingdom. It joins the intellectual functions with the field of sensation. Shin is the 31st path of Wisdom and is called the Perpetual Intelligence and carries the ideas of "continuance", "indefinite extension" and "perpetual time." Esoteric Astrology assigns Pluto to Shin. This card represents the Spiritual Fire, the Animating Principle. The numerical value of the Shin is 300.

THE SEVEN DOUBLES

Beth [B] is the first of the seven double letters and means house. The double letters tell the story of the holy and averse heptad. They depict the antithesis to which human life is exposed. Beth, being first among the doubles as well as first in the creation of the world, depicts the antithesis of life and death.

Beth is the 12th path of Wisdom and connects Kether — the Crown, with Binah — Understanding. It is called the Intelligence of Transparency or Light. The function implied is that of a transparent medium for the passage of light, that light being the Limitless Light concentrated in Kether.

The Esoteric Astrology assigns the planet Mercury to Beth. Mercury is also the Alchemical attribute of Beth. The numerical value of Beth is 2, signifying duplication, repetition.

Gimel [G] is the second of the seven double letters and means camel. Gimel depicts the antithesis of peace and strife. Gimel is the 13th path of Wisdom, the Uniting Intelligence, or the Conductive Intelligence of Unity. It joins the 6th sephirah Tiphareth — Beauty, with the first sephirah Kether — the Crown. The basic function of consciousness symbolized by Gimel is recollection, memory and represents the memory and eternal self-recollection of The One I Am.

In Esoteric Astrology, Gimel corresponds to the Moon. Silver is the Alchemical metal associated with Gimel. The numerical value of Gimel is 3, representing multiplication, fecundity, growth. The key idea associated with Gimel is memory.

Daleth [D] is the third of the seven double letters and means door. Daleth depicts the antithesis of Wisdom and Folly. Daleth is the 14th path of Wisdom, the Luminous Intelligence. It joins the 2nd sephirah Chokmah — Wisdom, with the 3rd sephirah Binah — Understanding. The basic power of Daleth is the pattern-forming power of creative imagination. The power which shapes mind-stuff into form before the externalization of such mental patterns into things which are actually existing at the level of physical, tangible manifestation.

In Esoteric Astrology, Daleth corresponds to the planet Venus. Copper is the Alchemical metal associated with Daleth. The numerical value of the Daleth is 4, representing order, system, regulation. The key idea associated with the Daleth is imagination.

Kaph [K] is the 4th double and means hand (open). It depicts the antithesis of wealth and poverty.

Kaph is the 21st path of Wisdom called the Intelligence of Desirous Quest. It is the path connecting Chesed — Mercy, with Netzach — Victory. It is the link between memory and desire. Kaph is the path through which the eternal beneficence of the One influences the desire nature.

Kaph manifests in human consciousness as the power to comprehend the cyclic activity of the One Self.

In Esoteric Astrology, Kaph represents the planet Jupiter. The value of Kaph is 20. In Alchemy Kaph is assigned to the metal Tin. The Law represented by Kaph is the law of Rotation.

Peh [P] is the 5th double and means mouth. It depicts the antithesis of grace and sin.

Peh is the 28th path of Wisdom called the Exciting Intelligence. It is the path connecting Hod — Splendor with Netzach — Victory. It is the link between intellect and desire. Peh is the path through which desire and thought interact upon one another. Peh manifests in human personality as the power of will.

In Esoteric Astrology, Peh represents the planet Mars. The value of Peh is 80. In Alchemy Peh is assigned to the metal Iron.

Resh [R] is the 6th double and means face. It depicts the antithesis of fertility and sterility.

Resh is the 30th path of Wisdom called the Collective Intelligence. Resh is the path connecting Hod — Splendor with Yesod — Foundation. It is the link between the intellect and automatic consciousness. Resh is the path through which thoughts influence and shape the habit-mind. Resh manifests in human personality as the sense of self-image.

In Esoteric Astrology, the Resh represents the Sun. The value of Resh is 200. In Alchemy Resh is assigned to the metal Gold.

Tau [Th] is the 7th double and means mark. It depicts the antithesis of dominion and slavery. Tau is the Holy double and directs all the operations of the seven planets, and concurs therein.

Tau is the 32nd path of Wisdom called the Serving, or Administrative Intelligence. Tau connects Yesod — Foundation with Malkuth — Kingdom. It is the link between automatic consciousness and the body. It is the path through which the habit-mind influences all bodily activities. In human personality Tau serves as the contact point with the Divine Soul.

In Esoteric, Astrology Tau represents the planet Saturn. The value of Tau is 400. In Alchemy Tau is assigned to the metal Lead.

THE TWELVE SIMPLES

Heh [H] is the first simple and means window. Heh represents the organ of sight. Foresight and true Vision are the qualities expressed.

Heh is the 15th path of Wisdom, the Constituting Intelligence. It joins the 2nd sephirah Chokmah — Wisdom, to Tiphareth — Beauty, the 6th sephirah.

In Esoteric Astrology, Heh represents Aries, the Ram. The value of Heh is 5. In Alchemy Heh is assigned to the Active fire.

Vau [V] is the second of the twelve simples and means nail. Vau governs hearing and all true communication with the Holy Life-Breath, is accomplished by this power.

Vau is the 16th path of Wisdom, the Triumphant and Eternal Intelligence. Vau is the path joining the second sephirah Chokmah — Wisdom, to the fourth sephirah, Chesed — Mercy. Intuition is the power that Vau manifests in human consciousness.

In Esoteric Astrology, Vau represents Taurus, the Bull. The value of Vau is 6. In Alchemy Vau is assigned to the Passive earth.

Zain [Z] is the third simple and means sword. Zain governs the sense of smell and is what allows us to discern the operations of the Secret Fire.
Zain is the 17th path of Wisdom, the Intelligence of Sensation, the Disposing Intelligence. Zain is the path connecting Binah — Understanding, with Tiphareth — Beauty and marks the narrow way of attainment

traveled only by those who are Masters of Faith. In human consciousness Zain manifests as the ability to make fine distinctions and classify and arrange according to type.

In Esoteric Astrology, Zain represents Gemini, the Twins. The value of Zain is 7. In Alchemy Zain is assigned to the Equilibrating air.

Cheth [Ch] is the 4th simple and means fence. It governs speaking. Cheth represents the field of the personality.

Cheth is the 18th path of Wisdom, The Intelligence of the House of Influence. Cheth is the path connecting Binah — Understanding, with Geburah — Severity, the 5th path on the Tree of Life. Cheth brings the Instruction of the Cosmic Teacher into the sphere of Volition.

In Esoteric Astrology, Cheth represents Cancer, the Crab. The value of Cheth is 8. In Alchemy Cheth is assigned to the Active water.

Teth [T] is the 5th simple and means serpent. It rules the function of taste.
Teth is the 19th path of Wisdom called the Intelligence of the Secret of all Spiritual Activities. Teth is the path connecting Chesed — Mercy, with Geburah — Severity. Teth is the channel through which the eternal Self-recollection of the One influences the operations of undeviating Law. In human consciousness Teth is that power which determines in what way and by what means an individual finds pleasure and gratification.

In Esoteric Astrology, Teth represents Leo, the Lion. The value of Teth is 9. In Alchemy Teth is assigned to the Passive fire.

Yod [I,J,Y] is the 6th simple and means hand (closed) It governs coition, touch.

Yod is the 20th path of Wisdom called the

Intelligence of Will. Yod is the path connecting Chesed — Mercy, with Tiphareth — Beauty. Yod is the path whereby the beneficence and loving-kindness of the One Self finds expression through the central Ego. In human consciousness Yod manifests as the power of mutual attraction between bodies and is what governs their joining.

In Esoteric Astrology, Yod represents Virgo, the Virgin. The value of Yod is 10. In Alchemy Yod is assigned to the Equilibrating earth.

Lamed [L] is the 7th simple and means ox-goad. It governs working.

Lamed is the 22nd path of Wisdom called the Faithful Intelligence. Lamed is the path connecting Geburah — Severity with Tiphareth — Beauty. Lamed is the means whereby the Volition of the Primal One energizes the Ego and gives It the sense of will. In human consciousness Lamed manifests as the power to weigh and measure all things.

In Esoteric Astrology, Lamed represents Libra, the Scales. The value of Lamed is 30. In Alchemy Lamed is assigned to the Active air.

Nun [N] is the 8th simple and means fish. It governs locomotion, walking.

Nun is the 24th path of Wisdom called the Intelligence of Resemblance, or the Imaginative Intelligence. Nun is the path connecting Tiphareth — Beauty with Netzach — Victory. Nun is the path through which the Ego influences the desire nature. In human consciousness Nun is involved with the pro-creative drive.

In Esoteric Astrology, Nun represents Scorpio, the Scorpion. The value of Nun is 50. In Alchemy Nun is assigned to the Passive water.

Samek[S] is the 9th simple and means prop. It governs wrath.

Samek is the 25th path of Wisdom called the Intelligence of Probation or Trial. Samek is the path connecting Tiphareth — Beauty with Yesod — Foundation. Samek brings the influence of the Ego into the sphere of the automatic consciousness and is what allows the Ego to direct the habit-mind. In human consciousness Samek manifests as the yearning for higher wisdom.

In Esoteric Astrology, Samek represents Sagittarius, the Archer. The value of Samek is 60. In Alchemy Samek is assigned to the Equilibrating fire.

Ayin [O] is the 10th simple and means eye. It governs mirth.

Ayin is the 26th path of Wisdom called the Renewing Intelligence. Ayin connects Tiphareth — Beauty with Hod — Splendor. Through the path of Ayin, the Ego influences and directs the functions of the intellect. In human consciousness Ayin depicts the ability to manage the affairs of the material plane and gain stature in the world.

In Esoteric Astrology, Ayin represents Capricorn, The Goat. The value of Ayin is 70. In Alchemy Ayin is assigned to the Active earth.

Tzadi [Tz] is the 11th simple and means fish-hook. It governs meditation.

Tzadi is the 28th path of Wisdom called the Natural Intelligence. Tzadi joins Netzach — Victory with Yesod — Foundation. Tzadi brings the influence of the desire nature into the field of automatic consciousness and is what allows the desire nature to shape patterns of habitual response. In human consciousness Tzadi depicts the ability to see the true nature of all created things.

In Esoteric Astrology, Tzadi represents Aquarius, the Water-bearer. The value of Tzadi is 90. In Alchemy Tzadi is assigned to the Passive air.

Qoph [Q] is the 12th simple and means back of head. It governs sleeping.

Qoph is the 29th path of Wisdom called the Corporeal Intelligence. Qoph joins Netzach — Victory to Malkuth — Kingdom. Through the path of Qoph the desire nature influences the physical vehicle and causes it to conform to the desires so held. In human consciousness Qoph manifests as the inclination toward religion.

In Esoteric Astrology, Qoph represents Pisces, the Fish. The value of Qoph is 100. In Alchemy Qoph is assigned to the Equilibrating water.

ESOTERIC IMPLICATIONS OF MINOR ARCANA

Keep in mind when considering the esoteric significance of the cards that polarity determines affinity. Each card has a positive and/or a negative connotation.

WANDS

Ace: The principle of Kether, Divine Self, in the world of principles, the archetypal plane. Initiative.
Two: The principle of Chokmah, Divine Life, on the plane of abstraction. Dominion.
Three: The principle of Binah, Divine Mind, in the world of ideas. Established strength.
Four: The principle of Chesed, Memory, on the spiritual plane. Perfected work.
Five: The principle of Geburah, Volition, in the highest world. Competition.

Six: The principle of Tiphareth, Central Self, in Atziluth. Victory.
Seven: The principle of Netzach, Desire, residing on the spiritual plane. Valor.
Eight: The prin Nine: The principle of Yesod, The Vital Soul, in Atziluth. Preparedness.
Ten: The principle of Malkuth, The Body, on the plane of abstraction. Fullness of power.
King: The personification of the principle of Light.
Queen: The personification of the principle of subconsciousness, Divine Mind.
Knight: The personification of the principle of Ego, the Central Self.
Page: The personification of the principle of Bodies.

CUPS

Ace: The image of Kether, Divine Self, on the creative plane. Desire force.
Two: The image of Chokmah, Divine Life, on the plane of mental and emotional energy. Response to environment.
Three: The image of Binah, Divine Mind, on the creative plane. Enjoyment.
Four: The image of Chesed, Mercy, in Briah. Surfeit.
Five: The image of Geburah, Volition, on the plane of mental patterns. Defeated desire.
Six: The image of Tiphareth, Central Self, at the Briatic level. Betterment.
Seven: The Image of Netzach, Desire, on the creative plane. Illusion.
Eight: The image of Hod, Intellect, on the plane of mental and emotional energy. Instability.
Nine: The image of Yesod, Vital Soul, in Briah. Desire fulfilled. Ten: The image of Malkuth, Body, on the

creative plane. Excess.
King: The personification of the image of Light.
Queen: The personification of the image of Divine Mind.
Knight: The personification of the image of Central Self.
Page: The personification of the image of Bodies.

SWORDS

Ace: The activity of Kether, Divine Self, on the astral plane. Activity.
Two: The activity of Chokmah, Divine Life, in the formative world. Indecision.
Three: The activity of Binah, Divine Mind, In Yetzirah. Sorrow.
Four: The activity of Chesed, Memory, on the plane of thought. Rest.
Five: The activity of Geburah, Volition, on the astral plane. Defeat.
Six: The activity of Tiphareth, Central Self, in the formative world. Patience.
Seven: The activity of Netzach, Desire, in Yetzirah. Instability. Eight: The activity of Hod, Intellect, on the plane of thought. Mediocrity.
Nine: The activity of Yesod, Vital Soul, on the astral plane. Worry.
Ten: The activity of Malkuth, Body, in the formative world. Destruction.
King: The personification of the activity of Light.
Queen: The personification of the activity of Divine Mind. Knight: The personification of the activity of Central Self. Page: The personification of the activity of Bodies.

COINS / PENTACLES

Ace: The manifestation of Divine Self in the material world. Materiality.
Two: The manifestation of Divine Life in the world of name and form. Fluctuation.
Three: The manifestation of Divine Mind in Assiah. Constructiveness.
Four: The manifestation of Memory on the plane of physical existence. Management.
Five: The manifestation of Volition in the material world. Uncertainty.
Six: The manifestation of Central Self in the world of effects. Prosperity.
Seven: The manifestation of Desire on the physical plane. Loss.
Eight: The manifestation of Intellect in Assiah. Prudence.
Nine: The manifestation of Vital Soul in the material world. Harvest.
Ten: The manifestation of Body in world of name and form. Wealth.
King: The manifestation of the personification of Light.
Queen: The manifestation of the personification of Divine Mind.
Knight: The manifestation of the personification of Central Self.
Page: The manifestation of the personification of Bodies.
It is not within the scope of this present work to elaborate the Minor Arcana. The author has covered this subject in another writing — **Rose Light - The Birth of the Rose Man.**

ROSE-LIGHT ATTRIBUTIONS OF THE TAROT

Card	Traditional	Rose-Light	Hebrew Letter	Letter Meaning	Letter Number
0	The Fool	Microcosmos	Aleph	Ox	1
1	The Magician	Magus	Beth	House	2
2	High Priestess	Sophia	Gimel	Camel	3
3	Empress	Aima	Daleth	Door	4
4	Emperor	Adam	Heh	Window	5
5	Hierophant	The Oracle	Vau	Nail or Hook	6
6	Lovers	Harmonia	Zain	Sword	7
7	Chariot	Victory	Cheth	Fence	8
8	Strength	Fohat	Teth	Serpent	9
9	Hermit	Ipsissimus	Yod	Hand (open)	10
10	Wheel of Fortune	The Kingdom	Kaph	Hand (closed)	20
11	Justice	The Amen	Lamed	Ox Goad	30
12	Hanged Man	Endura	Mem	Water	40
13	Death	Libertare	Nun	Fish	50
14	Temperance	Architect	Samekh	Prop	60
15	Devil	The Archon	Ayin	Eye	70
16	Tower	Grace	Peh	Mouth	80
17	Star	Aeth	Tzaddi	Fish-hook	90
18	Moon	The Fourth Hour	Qoph	Back of Head	100
19	Sun	Corpus Christi	Resh	Head	200
20	Judgment	Sanctus	Shin	Tooth	300
21	World	Neshemah	Tau	Mark (Tau)	400

MICROCOSMOS/ 0

ABOUT THE AUTHOR

Born October 8, 1948 in New York City NY.

Melvin Harris became interested in esoteric studies at the age of eight. His first affiliation with an organization offering instructions on the Western Mystery Tradition began when he was twelve. Since that time he has remained active and continues to follow in that tradition.

Over these years he has studied, practiced and lived the teachings and methods covering aspects of the Western Mystery tradition including Hermeticism, Spiritual Alchemy, Qabalah, Tarot, Esoteric Christianity, Catharism and Gnosticism. In some instances he has received personal training and instruction regarding implementation of certain teachings.

He offers this work to all sincere seekers of Truth as a Light on the Path — as a help and guide. It is hoped that the reader will find here some words or ideas worth considering and perhaps even a help on his/her own journey toward self discovery.

The author has spent the last 55 years in developing the Rose Light method.

ROSE LIGHT

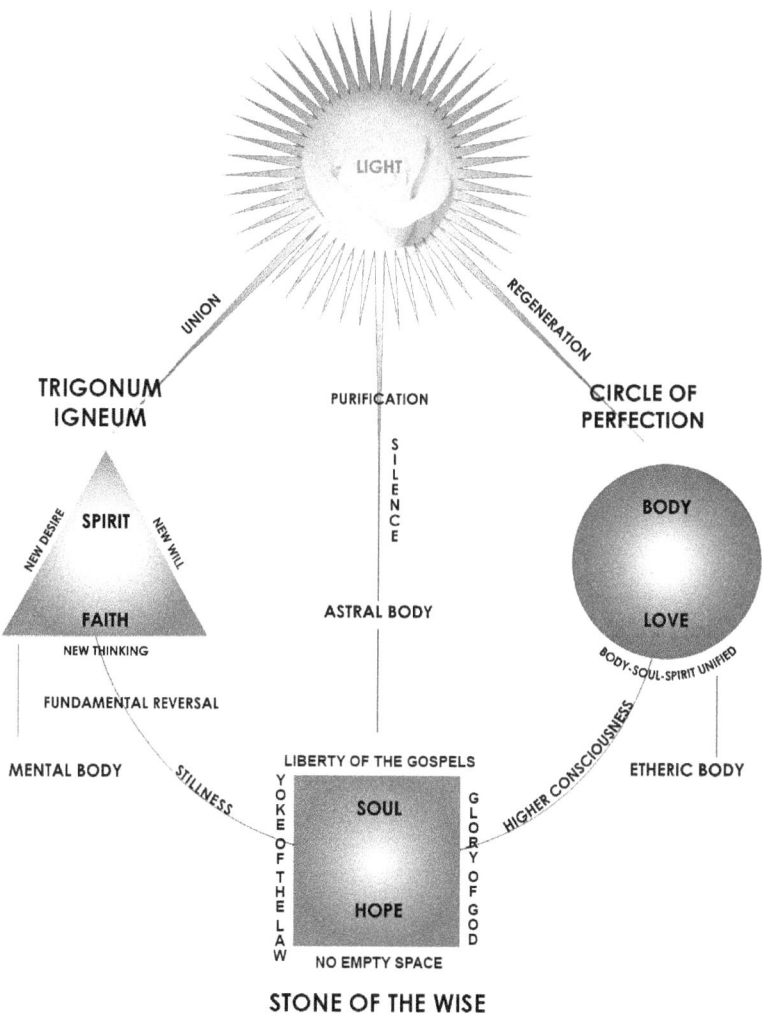

Key to the Gnostic Path of Tarot